Effective Altruism

--

The Same Old Altruism

By

Robert Villegas

Effective Altruism

--

The Same Old Altruism

By Robert Villegas

© Copyright 2023 by Robert Villegas. No part of this book can be reproduced without prior approval of the copyright holder or his legal representative.

ISBN: 9798864580059

Imprint: Independently published in the USA

indyboyaz@proton.me

Website: https://t.co/kQhv2C1OHC

Social Media Addresses

CloutHub @RobertVillegas
MeWe www.mewe.com/i/robertvillegas
Minds @Robertv1989
Gab @V4Vendata
Telegram @RobertVillegas
GETTR @V4Vendata
WIMKIN Robert Villegas
Freetalk45 @V4Vendata
X RobertVillegasJ

Table of Contents

- Introduction 5
- Creation versus Plunder 12
- What is Altruism? 18
- What is Effective Altruism? 28
- Understanding How Altruism Works 55
- Understanding How Selfish Living Works 68
- Kantianism, Menticide, and Altruism 72
- Altruism and Agoraphobia 84
- How do Dictatorships use Altruism to kill People? 86
- How Altruism and Guilt Cancel People 89
- Why Altruism Doesn't Work and Why it Always Fails 94
- ESG as an Altruist Scam 104
- Critical Race Theory as Altruism and Pseudo-Science 112
- Altruism as a Money Laundering Device 122
- Modern Philosophy as the Purveyor of Altruism 153
- The Call to Sacrifice as a Destroyer of Society . 166
- The Art of Killing Men 175
- Conclusion: Learning to Live Outside of Altruism 196
- About Robert Villegas 199

Introduction

> "Something is always happening. But when it happens, people don't always see it, or understand it, or accept it." – Nicholas Kazan

Most of us have heard the cliché: "Meet the new boss. same as the old boss". The same can be said about Peter Singer's effective altruism: "Meet effective altruism, same as the old altruism". Indeed, the problem with the new altruism is that it is *altruism*, nonetheless. This is because the fundamentals of effective altruism are the same as the fundamentals of primordial human sacrifice that began with the decimation of a scapegoat. Today's altruists seem to be realizing that the old altruism has never been effective. Now they are offering what they deem to be an "effective" version of the old altruism – that is different, new, and workable, so they say. The old altruism is dead; they think. Now it is time for something devastatingly new.

Effective altruism is a scam in the same way that primordial altruism convinced people it was moral for them to give up their values to the elites. Because of that real failure of the old altruism, they must rush to another way of moving history in their favor. It won't work, as Sam Bankman Fried has demonstrated.

It is interesting that modern philosophers, and university-trained CEOs, have adopted effective altruism. For them, it is the means for skimming the riches of successful corporations that have transformed themselves into social justice warriors. Effective altruism is a way for the elites to "fool" the people into retaining the barbarous policies that had stolen money from the productive middle class (in the past) and took aim directly at the profits of corporations. Seeing that the middle class has been decimated by centralized government they have realized that the "cash cow" of the average citizen has run out of "milk" (money). This has forced them to found a new scheme (or a new form of altruism) that will help them take the profits of *corporations*. By convincing CEOs that they don't deserve their profits, and should give them away, this new framework of corporate re-distribution, they think, they can continue to further decimate society through the new "cash cow" of corporate boardrooms. In fact, this new corporate bent of effective altruism assumes they can keep milking the cow indefinitely. In truth, corporations will not be able to continue being slaves because their profits will also run out in the long run. The pragmatists of stakeholder charitable giving will eventually run out of money. This is what happens when you think the end justifies the means.

To help us understand that effective altruism is really the same old altruism, we must understand the fundamental assumption of both altruism and effective altruism, and that is the idea that altruism is essentially good. Their new goal to do the most "good" possible ignores the obvious question: "what made altruism good in the first place". No effort is made by today's altruists to prove that taking away human value from the individual is good for mankind; they only *assume* that there is value in the practice of decimating the rights of individuals to their property.

Virtually all advocates of these two "isms" (altruism and effective altruism) assume that there is some benefit to giving. In other words, giving up values is supposed to actually improve people's lives, but it does not. Altruists ignore the fact that the more the altruist giver "contributes", the more he or she loses. Secondly, it ignores the fact that the receiver of re-distributed loot expects that his life will be benefited, but it is not.

In truth, effective altruism is a rebranding of altruism by means of a fraudulent connection of the old altruism to *logic and reason*. Yet, this connection has not been proven. Effective altruism will be as ineffective as the old altruism because it is based on the same premises that made the old altruism ineffective in the first place – property expropriation. As I will show, both altruism and effective altruism require a squandering of human value for the sake of those who cannot produce. Rather than investing their massive funds on building new values, new products and new profits, altruists squander corporate funds on wasteful projects that have little tangible result. These altruists hide their ineptitude by turning society into a fascist state that involves the "capture" of rich corporations that must invest their profits in social justice projects that inevitably fail.

Indeed, if the old altruism has been ineffective, this is proof that the new altruism will fail for the same reason. To drive this home, we must understand why the old altruism failed: The idea of taking from the productive in order to give to the unproductive is a failed notion. The morality of promiscuous giving is a call for plunder that leaves the "giver" decimated and disincentivized. Altruism takes so much from the individual that he and she cannot thrive. This same destruction of individual value in the old altruism, must surely also destroy the individual in effective altruism. Evidence and logic cannot be applied to an irrational form of morality, and it doesn't matter what you call it, altruism of any type cannot work. It squanders funds and then comes back for more. The giving never stops, and the spending never stops until society lies in rubble, millions are dead, and a new idea of altruism takes its place. The cherry on top for effective altruists is that everyone believes in altruism because the whole society is indoctrinated to keep the giving going ad infinitum.

For the first time in history, after decades of using altruism as a false promise, effective altruists have finally admitted that the old altruism didn't work. Now, the new altruism will be done right, they say, and it will save the world. This is because the new altruists are supposedly the right kind of people who can make it work. The hidden truth is that effective altruists, like the old altruists, don't know how to get rich except by convincing the productive individual to give them his money. Effective altruism is a get-rich-quick scheme deceptively designed to make the effective altruist a "good guy" who is only trying to help people. You will recall the old Marxist argument that Marxism has not worked because the people leading past Marxist movements were stealing from the working men, and NOW the next group of Marxists will do it right and create the real dream by stealing from the rich man – hence starting the next round of failed Marist policies. When these policies also fail, they promise a new round of Marxism that will work because the leaders are no longer killing people in mass quantities. When a new round of killing (or exploitation) occurs, then a new Marxism will emerge and so on and so on.

Likewise with altruism and effective altruism – it is yet another false promise of utopia that, like the old promises of utopia, are false and doomed to failure. The question to ask is "what will make effective altruism effective where the old altruism failed? They will not tell you this, because they don't know how to do things in reality. The real doers in society are the productive victims who have been beaten down by their altruistic masters. Where the old Marxists sought to confiscate factories and machines – which destroyed the incentive toward production in capitalism, effective altruism, rather than confiscating the machinery of production, the individuals, and the corporations, have taken a new step by "educating" *businesspeople* into believing they can contribute their production and profits and give the world hope.

The solution (for effective altruists) is to create a government/business alliance to cajole or nudge corporations, CEOs, and workers to use their profits – effectively. In other words, better management of productive corporations will bring about effective altruism and affluence. What corporations will do is work with government to solve human problems and bring about "social justice". The ox has found his mill, the corporations will be "captured" by government, and the individual who dissents will lose his job because of the surveillance done by the corporations that hired him.

What will cause the defeat of effective altruism? I think it is the notion that "words" or "thoughts" cannot really create reality. All effective altruists think that their "theory" of how to make altruism effective (for the first time in history) will magically create a new altruism in place of the old. This typical mistake has been seen throughout history during key conflicts where leftists, socialists, fascists, and communists have thought that *their* "theory", this time, can effect a change in society when it is nothing more than pure drivel. Just like pragmatism is not practical, effective altruism is not effective.

Creation versus Plunder

If philosophy moves history, then altruism is the fundamental moral principle that devastates history. This fact is what we have missed for thousands of years, and, as I will show, the influence of altruism has destroyed many societies.

We must understand the nature of man in order to see why altruism cannot work. Man, as a creative entity, must survive by means of reason. He cannot survive for long by plundering the values of others; this approach would engender retaliation and create conflict. He most certainly would be putting his own life in danger as is evidenced by the many plundering kings and dictators throughout history. They built castles, armies, made weapons and trained armed guards to protect them and their families. Yet, many despots found themselves attacked and often killed by citizens, other armies, and their own armies – they were even attacked and killed by their own armed guards, and their own children and grandchildren. Their plundering of others was not an effective means of survival.

Yet, despite the above, it was not kings (or dictators or government officials) who made the products that people needed. It was average, every day, cave men who made flint arrowheads and rock hammers. It was lowly, self-taught artisans who worked bronze, iron, red ochre, and gold into tools, art works, swords, and shields. It was uneducated carpenters and metal workers who made wheels and put them on carts and chariots. All of these products required the effective use of the human mind which means that creative man, surviving man, was able to make possible the practical uses that helped kings to thrive.

But the problem for "creative man" is not the fact of creation; the problem for all mankind is "plundering man", the man who would use force to take over the tools and products of survival and appropriate them for his own purposes. It was plundering man who enslaved creative man and brought about the social situation that throttled his ability to survive. It was plundering man who brought coercive social systems that included human sacrifice and the sacrificial rite.

Even today, plundering man thrives in the absence of limited government because there is no protector between the plunderer and the creative man. And since the creative man is not adept at defense (he is too busy creating), plundering man has the advantage of ambush, destruction, and attack. Plundering man thrives in anarchical, government-less situations and he does everything he can to create such situations.

Throughout history, creative man has been trying to find a way to stop plundering man. He finds himself most successful with limited constitutional governments. On the other hand, plundering man has found a variety of ways to gain and maintain his power of ambush, threat, and robbery. He has even enlisted the shaman to engender sacrifice and "giving" to make creative man feel guilty for wanting to keep what he produces.

In fact, plundering man (and the shaman) cannot exist without some scheme to control creative man. These schemes have consisted of altruism (moral force) outright force, murder, theft, enslavement, legalized theft (taxes) and legislated morality. In fact, in some cases, plundering man has convinced creative man that he is protecting him against other plunderers. In return for protecting him, he claims to only want a small tax in compensation. Inevitably, the small tax grows to ever larger proportions and plundering man uses his position of power to expropriate goods that give *him* a life of luxury while creative man works away in the dingy shop as a virtual slave.

Monarchy, the oldest form of coercive government, did not work after a time. People began complaining about plundering man's duplicity and corruption. Likewise, totalitarianism did not work and neither did theocracy. Over time, creative man has learned not to trust plundering man and he has developed various concepts that spell out clearly the proper relationship between man and his government. The result was constitutionally limited government. Through philosophers such as John Locke, ideas such as property and individual rights became part of an effort to create a limited government that treats plundering man as the criminal he is. Limited government does not give plundering man the power to rob creative man; it puts honest people in charge of government as protectors rather than criminals.

Once limited government was developed and implemented after the American Revolution, the economic result was capitalism. As long as proper government was in place, police could catch criminals, justice could prosecute them, and contracts could be enforced by the rule of law. Abundance and affluence were the result and once limited government was strong enough, it could regulate (make regular) society according to objective rules.

Needless to say, the idea of limited government was workable so long as people were not influenced by a subversive principle. Eventually that principle showed up in the form of altruism. Altruism subverted human freedom by demanding that men sacrifice their values (creative products) for the sake of others. As progressive philosophy advanced, the idea that government had the authority to take the income of some people by force (de facto) eliminated property rights. Altruism said, "from each according to his ability and to each according to his needs", and this principle, once accepted, began the process of taking more and more property from creative man. Plundering man had found a new way to continue his scheme to survive off of creative man.

For centuries, plundering man and the shaman have gotten away with making creative man feel guilty for keeping his values. As long as they were able to invoke guilt, they were able to subvert society and turn it into a mechanism for plundering re-distributed loot.

Little of this could have been accomplished in modern times without Marxism and re-distribution. Marx developed a false critique of capitalism and accused it of corruption, theft, exploitation, and slavery; none of which was true. He captured (for Marxism and leftism) the moral high ground that made it possible for the progressive movement to falsely assume the banner of fighting for certain "races", ethnic groups, the little guy, workers, the poor, the uneducated, and the indigent. Identity politics was born, and the progressives used it to divide individuals into warring groups/collectives they pretended to champion. This gave it the power it needed to dominate the political conversation, to continue stealing from creative man and to win the day against individual rights and "selfishness".

With individual rights and "selfishness" safely discredited, Marx and his minions (revolutionaries and Alinskyites), over decades, were able to masquerade as pragmatists who "knew" how to solve our problems. This "anti-ideology" left creative man without a defense while the progressives won the votes, establishing "democratic" systems that expropriated money from the rich. The result was decaying cities, economic decline and continued anti-capitalist rhetoric. The left proclaimed their "love" for the common man against the evil rich exploiters while the conservatives were pushed out as favoring the rich.

Even today, many conservatives and progressives stop reading my words because I am pointing out the plundering aspect of altruism, the philosophy upon which they base their plans for the demise of creative man. Conservatives and progressives are both altruists, one group, for God, and the other for the "beloved" state.

What is Altruism?

I first read the novel "Atlas Shrugged" by Ayn Rand during a two-week period at a military base where I was awaiting orders for my coming tour of duty. This was in late November 1966. I remember this because I had recently been assigned kitchen duty on Thanksgiving Day.

I had previously asked my father to go to a book store in Indianapolis and buy a copy of the book to send me. The paperback edition was over 1000 pages but, while reading it, there was a particular chapter I skipped because it was a long speech given by the protagonist (to explain why he was protesting government policies). I felt I could read the rest of the book and then get back to this skipped chapter after I had arrived at my duty base.

Of course, I was partially wrong about this. In fact, I was only twenty years old during the Vietnam War era. A couple of years later, I finally read that skipped chapter. As a young man, I had not, at that time, known very much about the field of philosophy and had made a promise to myself to further delve into Rand's philosophy through other Objectivist materials as well as the works of Aristotle.

I must admit that I had been an avid reader of the works of Aristotle who had been recommended to me by a philosophy student from Butler University (who had also recommended Atlas

Shrugged) when I was a mere 14-year-old boy. I had already purchased an entire set of historically significant books on philosophy by that time as well.

When I was 20, the Selective Service decided to draft me into the military. By November of 1966, I had already completed Army Basic Training, and had just completed Radio Teletype training at Fort Gordon, GA. A few days after finishing *"Atlas Shrugged"*, I received my orders for Korea (I would not be going to Vietnam). A stroke of luck!

Since those early days, I have managed to read Atlas at least three times and went through the entire text of Galt's speech that I discovered to be crucial to my understanding of Rand's philosophy.

I have spent most of my life learning the philosophy of Objectivism, listening to its lecturers, and admiring its heroes. Over those many years, the more I learned, the more I was convinced that it is the right philosophy for "living on earth". I still strive to be an Objectivist hero if only in my mind.

Ayn Rand, who started as a commercial writer in the movie industry, thought that her philosophy could only capture the world through the universities (if "capture" is the right word). She thought, I believe, that the universities were the ivory towers, the pinnacles from which the best ideas of the arts, politics, and business worlds were held.

Rand was clear that modern philosophy, the driving influence in the world during her lifetime, was in a dismal state. David Hume (and other philosophers) had laid the foundation for philosophical decline by declaring that necessity did not exist, that cause-and-effect could not be seen. These ideas had put the world into a tailspin and a downward descent. To solve the problems declared by Hume, Kant promised to solve the "problem" of induction.

In fact, you can't solve the problem of induction by accepting Hume's terms; you must challenge them at their core, and this is what Rand and her student, Dr. Leonard Peikoff, accomplished during my lifetime. Rand reminded us that the connection between cause-and-effect could indeed be ascertained; that Hume was wrong, and that Kant only pretended to solve the problem. He left mankind in the lurch between not seeing and not knowing.

This problem, the problem of induction, was crucial to the history of the world. Hume had set man on the path of being unable to "know" and Kant only made the road clear for indeterminacy. There was very little difference between Hume and Kant in a fundamental sense.

For Rand and her champion Aristotle, induction was not invalidated by the absence of necessity.

There was no such absence. Induction and observation of the facts of reality were cornerstones of Rand's philosophy.

One thing I like about Objectivism is that it hasn't changed over the years. Objectivism is the philosophy of Ayn Rand and no other person. It is her words and her words only that make it what it is. Other people who are knowledgeable of Rand's philosophy can help you understand it, but they are not adding anything to the fundamentals of Objectivism; with the exception of Peikoff, they are teachers, not philosophers.

Galt's Speech (and her philosophy) were, in effect, answers to both religion and modern philosophy. This also includes philosophers such as Descartes, Hume, Kant, Pierce, Dewey, and even Marx, to name a few. I have also taken several courses on the history of philosophy to broaden my understanding about religion and modern philosophy.

Through all of this study of Objectivism and modern philosophy, I saw that the key feature that needed to be challenged throughout history is the moral philosophy of altruism. Altruism is the BIG LIE of our time. The crucial question is "how has altruism managed to insinuate itself into our culture and done so much damage to our institutions and lives?" In fact, my subsequent readings of the fathers of religion and modern philosophy corroborate Rand's views on altruism and the devastating consequences this moral philosophy has had on our lives. The answer to that question makes up the basis of this book. Everyday, I am reminded of the prevalence of altruism and its hold on the moral life of mankind. I look at the Amazon ratings and misguided reviews of some of my books and attribute them to the influence of altruism as a staple of modern society. Men just can't bring themselves to read words that challenge the moral philosophy they largely accept on faith alone – without regard for the real consequences in dead bodies and rubble. Those reviews are wrong because altruism is wrong. In this book, and several other books I have written, I try to show why altruism is having devastating consequences in society.

Since I am an intellectual foe of altruism, to the charlatans preaching altruism today, I do not understand morality and what the world needs. Most of these foes among scholars, religious leaders and Marxists maliciously assume man to be a sinful, egotistic creature, and altruism (the giving up of value) is the only moral philosophy that will undo the pull of selfishness in society.

In fact, we live in a world dominated by the Kantian influence, by the belief that man is intellectually incompetent, that guilt is the only way to control him, and that it is the job of society's institutions to manipulate him for the benefit of mankind, or God, or history, or the collective of the moment. If this doesn't prove the power of guilt to destroy lives, nothing can. This guilt is the animating principle for altruism and effective altruism.

I declare that it is the scoundrels of altruism who represent evil in the world. It is the influence of these scoundrels that keeps honest and innocent "believers" captive to the tenets of human sacrifice. Most people do not question altruism because they have been indoctrinated into thinking that reason and egoism are false, and that sacrifice of the individual will actually benefit society. This last is the premise I challenge.

Yet, I declare that these scoundrels are part of the battle against man and his mind. In order to defeat that evil, one must be willing to fight it on the foundation that holds the mind to be incompetent in the world; and that man needs his mind (and the products of his mind) to live a truly moral life. Egoism and individualism are the foundations of morality, not its enemies. One must shout that it is time to look at the prevalent altruistic moralities in the world and question them, criticize them, analyze their histories and be unafraid of making people angry. And so here we are.

I ask the reader to reconsider his moral views and especially his view that altruistic self-sacrifice is good for man and the world. Ask yourself if this view is true and come along with me for this evaluation of history's most consequential moral atrocity, altruism, and its child effective altruism. Perhaps we can save the world and avert the dangerous consequences that will surely come.

Altruism is a historical and philosophical descendant of ritual human sacrifice. The key premises of primitive altruism include:
- Impending catastrophe or disaster that threatens the collective or tribe.
- Nationalism.
- The presumed need for a victim whose death will appease the catastrophizing entity.
- The sacrificial rite and the murder of sacrificial victims.
- The celebration over the catastrophe's supposed diminishment.

Today, the sacrificial right of primitive (ritual) altruism has been altered to appeal to modern sensibilities and has become modern philosophy:
- The phenomenal and noumenal realms that destroy the mind and keep it from ascertaining reality.
- Emergency or potential disaster that threatens society.
- Utopianism, socialism, communism, and progressivism.

- The need for the individual (victim) to give up values for the sake of others in society – the moral imperative.
- The ritual re-enactment of human sacrifice (drama or ritual dance)
- The transfer of value to the state or religion.
- Guilt assuagement (human psychology) through indoctrination and gaslighting.

Today, one of the most anti-mind forms of altruism is called effective altruism, which is an effort to rebrand altruism into something associated with reason and logic. Effective altruism wrongly assumes that altruism (sacrifice) is "good morality" without any supporting evidence. It asserts that everyone should "want" to sacrifice for others without explaining "why" altruism is correct, how it works, and why it will not foster the same societies and genocides that it brought about during the last several centuries. Rationalism itself is a disconnection (through faith) of the mind from reality. Religion and modern philosophy both elevate subjectivism in society and destroy moral living. Religion gave us Jesus, the ultimate human sacrifice, while modern philosophy (skepticism, empiricism, sensualism, and nominalism) gave us "duty" (the categorical imperative). Both concepts of morality steal true morality in action and replace it with ritual human sacrifice to appease either God or Society. Therefore, it is not possible to connect altruism to reality by reference to reason and objective knowledge.

Reason and rationalism are incompatible. The only real option is to repudiate rationalism and altruism (as well as collectivism) and replace them with individualism, reason, and logic. Only then can we accomplish a true reality-based morality and adhere to egoism and self-interest. Reason can never countenance a moral philosophy that denies reason. The framers of effective altruism are smoking a pipe dream. Effective altruism is an effort, so to speak, to put a band aid on human sacrifice by assuming that the disastrous history of altruism can be corrected by a focus on reality. In fact, altruism divorces the mind from reality and tries to cover it up with reason – which is an impossibility, a pipe dream. Over the centuries the sacrificial rite has brought violence and hatred toward the individual while receiving praise as the bringer of peace and love. The murderous aspects of human sacrifice have been overtly "minimized" and turned into something less offensive than ritual murder. Their only remnants today are found in genocide, the mass murder of individuals. Today, through the notion of collectivism, their most common expression is taxation, monetary inflation, and the sacrifice of human values by productive individuals. Today, millions of individuals are working for free to pad the coffers that enable politicians to launder money and steal elections. The politicians get rich while the workers pay higher prices for the things they need. Progressives of both left and right are the enemies of the individual.

It has never been asked (throughout history) "why altruism has moved from murderous human sacrifice to charitable giving and taxation." Certainly, most modern forms of altruism are less violent than the original human sacrifice found in tribalism, yet still there are forms of human sacrifice that kill people. These include racism, genocide, war, and mass murder. Until altruism is removed as a factor in society, we can never advance beyond barbarism.

If you want to cure society from the doldrums created by altruism (poverty), the best way to do it is to introduce intellectual independence. By liberating the mind, you build up a stronghold of new ideas that leads to a creative movement defined by wealth, better products, and life-serving economic results. Once the independent individual is liberated, you will enhance free thought, free speech, and productive capitalism. Liberation protects men from the confiscation of their values and property.

What is Effective Altruism?

Effective altruism is altruism, the same moral philosophy that has been practiced for centuries. Effective altruism repudiates original altruism because Marxists are trying yet another scheme to help them loot society. They have realized that original forms of altruism do not work, and that altruism might be on the verge of being dismissed as a moral philosophy. Effective altruism not only repudiates the inefficacy of ancient altruism but fails in exactly the same way that it has failed for centuries.

To hide their true motives of looting society, they have found a new way of collectivizing people around a "new" movement called the effective altruism movement. This so-called movement seeks to appeal to the better natures of people by motivating them to give away their riches to charity. Essentially the looters "bank" their moneys in charities (a euphemism for money laundering). By leveraging their stolen loot through charitable giving, they take advantage of centuries of altruistic indoctrination, unmonitored corruption, and payoffs, that keep them rich and in power. In fact, they use mere words to divert huge amounts of money that will supposedly make altruism "effective". This last is the LIE – effective altruism is a money laundering scheme and nothing more.

The utter stupidity of this concept shows how vulnerable people are to charlatans who cover their nefarious activities under a blanket of "doing good". When they hear that giving your money away to charity is a "good" investment, they rush to signal their virtuous intent by throwing their money into crypto currencies or some other scams built up into investment bubbles they can sell short on. The idea of effective altruism is nothing more than a "bubble" being built up to rob people of their money. This is a scam artist's dream. Where a smart investor would quickly realize that investing the proceeds from his productive work would be more "effective" if he used those funds to create new products and services, create new productive jobs, new infrastructure and new inventions, effective altruists invest the funds in areas that will essentially squander the money (as happened with Sam Bankman-Fried's donations into the Democratic Party).

"Effective altruism is based on a very simple idea: we should do the most good we can. Obeying the usual rules about not stealing, cheating, hurting, and killing is not enough, or at least not enough for those of us who have the great good fortune to live in material comfort, who can feed, house, and clothe ourselves and our families and still have money or time to spare. Living a minimally acceptable ethical life involves using a substantial part of our spare resources to make the world a better place. Living a fully ethical life involves doing the most good we can."[1]

Notice that, for starters, they only want to skim from you the money you "supposedly" don't need, the money that you don't know how to spend, the surplus money you are looking around for something to do with. Don't be fooled – that is merely a promise to get their foot in the door and rob you blind. The true reality of altruism is to make you a full altruist, someone who knows that in order to be moral he must give up everything for others (with the expectation that they will give up everything for him). This is what altruism has always been, thievery.

This quote is intended to pull the wool over your eyes. As with the old altruism, they never mention the damage done to productive people, and only mention the supposed benefit to unproductive people.

We must point out that effective altruism is being put forward by intellectual lightweights, people who are using effective altruism to get rich. Ostensibly, their approach is to obtain funds from people who believe in altruism and use (or launder) that money to mostly progressive social programs. It is clear that effective altruists are corporatists and fascists who use effective altruism to collect huge amounts of funds they use

---

[1] The Most Good You Can Do: How Effective Altruism is Changing Ideas About Living Ethically" by Peter Singer

to launder among themselves, in short, creating empty giving schemes to each other. Here is a short history from Wikipedia:

"Beginning in the late 2000s, several communities centered around altruist, rationalist, and futurological concerns started to converge, such as:

"The evidence-based charity community centered around GiveWell, including Open Philanthropy, which originally came out of GiveWell Labs but then became independent.

"The community around pledging and career selection for effective giving, centered around the Giving What We Can and 80,000 Hours organisations.

"The Singularity Institute (now MIRI) for studying the safety of artificial intelligence, the Future of Humanity Institute studying topics such as existential risk, and the LessWrong discussion forum, which focuses on rationalism.

In view of this "history" we must ask what does doing the most good mean in a practical sense? How much evidence and reason is applied to identifying the most good. From what we can tell, the people and groups that make up the movement of effective altruism are not logical and evidence based as they claim. These terms appear to be buzzwords to fool people about their charity industrial complex that portrays itself as a communitarian group built on human sacrifice.

What does doing the "most good" for people mean? In fact, the term is ambiguous – it cannot be measured, and I suspect it is deliberately vague in order to cover up the fact that not all of the funds confiscated are being spent on "needy" people, but are being "invested" into high technology apps (that will make them uber-rich) to be distributed to every citizen and create more "convenience" for "captured" individuals who must submit to the new globalist model based on technocracy and AI[2]. This enables them to determine capital flows in society that trap people into schemes that the effective altruists control. It sounds an awful lot like the World Economic Forum which seeks the business/government alliance (fascism). This is actually what they mean when they use buzzwords such as "evidence and reason" to measure the most good for their captured slaves. Apparently, they are not using evidence and reason to measure the most *harm* done to people by effective altruism. It is productive people who will be trapped into buying what they are supposed to buy in order to make government sponsored Apps that will make them all (politicians and monopolized industries) rich. In a sense, this makes effective altruism into a religion that is disconnected from reality, that sees altruism as a sort of conceptual god-being that has

---

[2] Artificial Intelligence

total moral authority over captured customers. I call it "forced loyalty marketing".

One could say that the existence of effective altruism, as a religion, was created by a loss of moral authority by both religion and human sacrifice (altruism). Today, men are beginning to challenge the left, the Marxists, and the totalitarian minded globalists – they are beginning to quietly say "No" to the calls for collective joining and collective sacrifice that has decimated numerous civilizations throughout history. Most people don't know why they hate the whining talking heads of the WEF and Open Society Foundations, but they feel there is something sleazy and "begging" about these people and they don't think they can quietly go along with all the calls for "community service" and social agitation on behalf of men who, mostly, did not earn their billions, who used government to create their monopolies, and who have the effrontery to tell others that their lives should happily belong to them. Once men realize that these men do not bring "the science", the technologies, and the utopia they have always promised, they will merely fade away like the Starnes family in Ayn Rand's novel Atlas Shrugged. All it took for the Starnes heirs to lose their particular call to sacrifice was one person who said, "I'm going to stop the motor of the world". It is time for people to start questioning their religion of the altruist god.

To be clear, every dollar taken from a productive citizen is one less dollar he can spend to improve his own life. Additionally, the idea that most people have massive amounts of surplus earnings to give to others is seldom true, and to think so is an insult to people trying to make ends meet. There is simply not that much surplus money to go around, especially considering economic conditions today.

In truth, the creator of surplus wealth is always the better person to decide what to do with that surplus – the creator of wealth is always going to be the best person to know how to use his wealth to create even more wealth – giving that money away to someone who will likely waste it is not effective – in fact, the person who does not earn wealth is likely the worst person to know how to invest the money.

One false assumption is that doing good for others is a moral imperative. There is no reason to believe this. What logic supports this? The altruist's goal here is to hope that others will believe that doing good for others is a requirement of living. So, they insinuate the truth of this without proof and then declare they have found the best way to do it. Do you believe they are the best people to know how you should spend your money? I don't trust George Soros or Klaus Schwab with my money.

We should ask about the meaning of this statement by Singer: "Obeying the usual rules about not stealing, cheating, hurting, and killing is not enough, or at least not enough for those of us who have the great good fortune to live in material comfort, who can feed, house, and clothe ourselves and our families and still have money or time to spare."

Perhaps professor Singer can open up his checking and savings accounts and give all of his surplus money to the needy. Needless to say, Singer has it wrong. Not stealing, not cheating, not hurting, and not killing implies a very low moral standard. In a sense, Singer's description is not about morality but about anti-morality. Not doing something is omission not commission. Morality should be about doing positive things and engaging in virtuous activities that foster life – your life with your money. It is irrelevant that morality consists of not stealing, cheating, hurting, and killing. Morality consists of defining values and moving forward positively to create or acquire them.

This betrays Singer's mindset because he sees morality at a superficial level that does not express a true moral code (based upon evidence and reason). Further, living in material comfort does not make altruism desirable by any means. In fact, very few of us live in material comfort today, and doing so does not satisfy us as Singer implies. He assumes that people everywhere are looking for ways to use their income to help people, implying that there is a market for effective altruism. Some of them may want to help the Little League team, for instance. But effective altruism is not the only choice for men nor even the most effective way to accomplish something they want. And effective altruists don't want you to have a choice – it is their moral imperative or else. You must be an effective altruist if you want to keep the job they own. Their way or the highway, so to speak.

To assume that altruism is the only good morality is false. Other virtues can include self-interest, egoism, and planning to buy something that requires a longer-term plan. Living creatively and reaching for more material comfort, more wealth, and more happiness, should be the moral starting point, not looking around for ways to squander money by spending it on others.

When people learn how to establish material comfort, they may not look for ways to give up their values for others. Instead, they may look around for ways to be happier, have children, and care for their children in ways that are more beneficial for them. Spending surplus money to make the lives of your children better would not be effective altruism, but it would be to *your* self-interest. And it might even create sustainable work for someone who is now poor. Should the man with surplus wealth forego helping his children because effective altruists demand his money? How could that be more effective than keeping your wealth and spending it (or investing it) to help yourself? You know what they say about the achievement of self-sufficiency. Altruism and "effective" altruism do not give increased value to productive people; but rather, they rob them of their happiness, and it is the injunction to sacrifice more that ruins lives. Contrary to the common belief, altruism, giving up values, is not the "go to" morality once the individual learns how to be affluent. The "go to" morality is more of what made him or her affluent in the first place – more egoism. The virtue of productiveness (or should I say the virtue of selfishness) comes with pride, self-esteem, and volition. Once an individual's life becomes full of virtue, he or she learns the value of virtuous action, and realizes that abundance (in virtuous action) is a positive reflection of living a good, egoistic life. If more virtue makes the individual more affluent, then giving up values would likely be resisted by the truly moral person. In effect, he would rebel against the notion of giving up his or her values.

The final line of the quote above, "Living a fully ethical life involves doing the most good we can", is, on the contrary, truer within the context of keeping one's values, not giving them away to people who would squander them. In fact, a truly ethical life can only lead to an understanding of what makes morality possible, and that is egoism and self-esteem.

A quote from Magnus Vinding exposes a false premise of "Effective Altruism": "Effective altruism is the ideal of helping others as much as possible." Strangely, this expression exposes the truth that virtually every philosopher and religious scholar evades – the truth that ancient altruism has never worked. They thought, if only subconsciously, that their specific forms of altruism were not effective at all. That is why they kept demanding more and more sacrifice – whenever a program or scheme failed, they knew they could only ask for more money.

The god father of effective altruism tells us: "Effective altruism is the project of using evidence and reason to figure out how to benefit others as much as possible, and taking action on that basis." – William MacKaskill[3]

In truth, effective altruism is a criticism of ancient altruism. Effective altruists imply that ancient altruism has fallen short and is now ready to be "saved" by a new definition of the concept. In fact, effective altruists are oblivious to evidence

---

[3] Quote taken from "Effective Altruism: How Can We Best Help Others?" by Magnus Vinding

and reason because, if you advocate evidence and reason, you cannot advocate a ludicrous and illogical concept such as altruism. Effective altruists have never learned that evidence and reason are actually required for egoism, production, and reason, not for a willing sacrifice of values. No reasonable person would ever think that altruism could be bolstered by evidence and reason.

What does it mean to say that effective altruism is about how to help people in the best possible ways? Does this not imply that men, throughout history, have wrongly practiced altruism in ways that are not the best possible? What features of ancient altruism made it ineffective (We will discuss this issue in the following chapter)?

One might be surprised to learn that laissez faire capitalism, during the industrial revolution, created the most wealth in the history of the world. It elevated the poor and brought them into the middle and upper classes. Capitalism did *not* create poor people; it was the anti-capitalists, the Marxists and communists who floundered in inefficacy (and killed millions of productive people), both morally and politically; it was not the capitalists. Capitalism provides none of the poverty that altruism needs to alleviate – there is no need for altruism in a capitalist society despite what the altruists and socialists tell us. There is less poverty in capitalism and the poverty that exists is actually caused by the interference of government into capitalism. Socialism causes poverty, not capitalism.

It is also capitalism that brought evidence and reason into the modern world, not altruism. This meant that capitalism was more effective than altruism at producing better products and affluence. To declare that altruism, the sacrifice of the individual, is better than capitalism, is a truly ludicrous idea that defies evidence and reason. If men want a better society, they should run as fast as possible to capitalism and individual rights.

The proof that capitalism produces abundance is there for all to see, despite the fact that capitalism has never existed in a full laissez faire system, and despite the fact that the power to produce has been diluted by Marxist intellectuals, high taxation, confiscation of property, government regulations, etc. (all proposed by altruists for centuries). In fact, were it not for the interventions of altruists into the capitalist system, there is every reason to conclude that capitalism would have eliminated poverty long ago if it had been left free of socialist and fascist interventions.

One could say that capitalism was not as effective as it could have been, were it not for the machinations, deceptions, indoctrination, and gaslighting of Marxist and progressive intellectuals who have sought to steal capitalist production. We could say that altruism, even effective altruism, has had its day and it is time for a new idea (full capitalism) if we want to truly use evidence and reason. Capitalism, the bastion of freedom, trade, and individualism, has still not had its day in the sun.

Effective altruists, like many progressives and pragmatists, claim to adhere to evidence and reason. Yet, reason cannot be mustered as foundational to an unreasonable project to re-distribute money, and this is because redistribution is an unreasonable act. Effective altruists cannot, in reason, justify taking values from people who would not otherwise give them up freely. In fact, they can't, in reason, support taking the values of people for *their* own designs. The claim that they hold evidence and reason as top values is to use these concepts as cynical punch lines.

Effective altruists use *these* concepts (evidence and reason) today, and tomorrow they will use other concepts (such as faith and religion) as needed. As pragmatists, they play a game of conceptual "whack-a-mole" cynically using concepts to suit themselves, and then discarding them when they have achieved their purpose. They evaluate reality on the basis of public opinion polls and the idea that perception is reality. Everywhere they use shifting values and smooth talk to blend in with society and make people think their values are theirs. In truth, they are pragmatist cynics who will take up any values so long as they can use them to fool people about their motives. For them, the end justifies the means, and this applies to the glowing phrases found in numerous books that cavalierly praise the sloppy thinking of effective altruism. Evidence and reason? Hardly.

I'm reminded of the fact that effective altruists, even the CEOs of top corporations, are not economic wizards. They have never been able to create abundance by investing in giveaway programs and they survive by running companies that are essentially on remote control. I'm also reminded of SBF (Sam Bankman Fried), an effective altruist, who used his profits to engage in wasteful money laundering schemes that re-distributed money from him to Ukraine, and to the Democratic party. He is decidedly not a capitalist and, as an effective altruist, he has proven his ignorance. He is not a genius of anything; he is a fool running on the fumes left over from what little capitalism is left in our society.

In truth, effective altruists like Peter Singer draw a false distinction between a "minimally effective ethical life" and a "fully moral life". For the effective altruist, a minimally effective ethical life is a compromised life between good and evil and a fully moral life is what we should call a completely sacrificial life. The falsehood here is that neither of these ethical choices can make a person moral. Morality comes from effective capitalism, capital investment, profits, and success, not from giving everything away.

For effective altruism, there are only two types of morality. They are 1) the moral compromiser who is morally inconsistent, and 2) the human sacrifice who gives his total production to others. Any person who lives a so-so moral life (number 1) keeps some of his values and only reluctantly gives up other values, while the fully sacrificial person (number 2) cannot survive because he has no money left to pay for personal needs. He would be like Francis of Assisi who lived a completely ascetic life.

These two "split" models of effective altruism expose the truth that human sacrifice (full altruism) makes man into a creature who yearns to be eaten by man. It assumes that the fully moral life (the fully sacrificial life – number 2) must be always sacrificing, while the minimally effective (number 1) moral life is a moral compromiser who must feel guilty for not sacrificing enough. Note the contradiction here: altruism destroys the possibility of a self-interested morality.

Altruism is (and was) ineffective throughout history because it required that producers (under force or willingly) give up their values, which requirement removed the hope of living freely without interference of government. Altruism was ineffective because it could not steal enough money to effectively improve the lives of people. It diminished the lives of producers and further impoverished the lives of the unproductive. There is no way to make "giving" more effective.

This is because once re-distribution started to take over society, it was subject to the law of diminishing returns. The more altruists stole from society, the more the poor proliferated while the rich began to disappear. You cannot have consumption without first creating production and in order to have production, you need to liberate individuals to be fully self-interested, not tie them up and steal their belongings. This is why altruism is not effective and why it can never be effective. Once effective altruists are done spending (re-distributing) all the money they collect, they invariably need more. As I have written before, there will never be enough sacrificing in the world made by altruism. The amount of human energy needed to help all of the poor is so immense; altruism can never eradicate poverty. It can only create more poverty – until the productive men are gone.

With effective altruism, the productive individual must work harder and harder to come up with the surplus needed for centralized government. What the government can't extort it takes from inflated currencies that also clandestinely steal from the productive. Using their own paradigm, the pond to which the sacrificer must go to save the drowning child keeps getting farther and farther away – despite the assurances of effective altruists. Not only must the savior of the child have to do more and more work, but the amounts of money needed to get him to the pond grows larger and larger.[4]

---

[4] "In a famous 1972 article, "Famine, Affluence, and Morality," philosopher Peter Singer compared global poverty to a child drowning in a pond:
""[I]f it is in our power to prevent something very bad from happening, without thereby sacrificing
anything morally significant, we ought, morally, to do it. An application of this principle would be as follows: if I am walking past a shallow pond and see a child drowning in it, I ought to wade in and pull the child out. This will mean getting my clothes muddy, but this is insignificant, while the death of the child would presumably be a
very bad thing."
""If we ought to prevent something very bad from happening whenever we can do so without sacrificing anything morally significant, then we also ought to spend much of our lives and wealth on rescuing people from starvation and disease:"
""It makes no moral difference whether the person I can help is a neighbor's child ten yards from me or a Bengali whose name I shall never know, ten thousand miles away. . . [We should make] no distinction between cases in which I am the only person who could possibly do anything and cases in which I am just one among millions in the
same position."
""Instead of buying a Starbucks coffee once a week, you could save that money – about $200 over the course of a year – and give it to a charity that saves lives. It's morally wrong to buy Starbucks coffee when there are people dying around the world. Letting someone die so that you can enjoy Starbucks is like letting a child drown rather than getting your suit muddy."
""It doesn't matter that most other people aren't living up to their moral obligations. Bystanders' failure to save a drowning child doesn't relieve you of a duty to save that child. If you can save a life without sacrificing anything morally significant, you must"".
"What should we make of this argument? The analogy between saving someone from extreme poverty and saving a drowning child seems strong. Millions of people around the world die young (or at birth) due to disease and malnutrition. We in affluent countries spend much of our wealth on luxuries. In fact, we eat too much and watch too much TV. Can't we afford to spend a lot of that wealth on helping save others' lives? And if we can afford it, don't we have an obligation to do it?" Source:

"Singer's argument faces two main difficulties. First, he thinks it's obvious that consuming luxuries isn't morally significant. But is that right? Perhaps having your once-a-week Starbucks can be as morally significant as saving a life, strange as that may sound. Second, he thinks saving poor people's lives is about as simple as wading into a pond and dragging a drowning child out of danger. But in fact, it might be a lot more complicated."[5]

As I have shown, the sacrificial victim who provides the funds for effective altruism will eventually realize that his executioner is not a nice person, that he is stealing from him, while leading a very nice life. (See Joe Biden). In fact, when effective altruists arrive to the point when there is no more money left to loot (no more children drowning in the pond), the last person they will save is the provider of the funds. What happens when that person stops working? It is at this point when genocide and slave labor camps are needed (to save society). Yes, Stalin was an effective altruist.

Effective altruists even have the audacity to tell us that even if the money taken is wasted, we should be ok with that because *some* people are saved

---

https://www.e3ne.org/is-poverty-like-a-pond/#:~:text=In%20a%20famous%201972%20article%2C%20%E2%80%9C%20Famine%2C%20Affluence%2C,morally%20significant%2C%20we%20ought%2C%20morally%2C%20to%20do%20it.

[5] Ibid

(talk about "effective"). In fact, they completely ignore the harm to the children of the parents whose money is taken from them. They can't even promise that they, themselves, will be effective. That's what you get for voting for effective altruist politicians (of both left and right).

I would also like to point out that effective altruism is *not* evidence- or reason-based. It is supposed to be effective, but it is not. This can be discerned when you hear that government programs (or even corporate programs) are "investments" in the community. This lie can be discerned when we see that an investment is supposed to be returned along with a profit (interest). On the other hand, effective altruists do not expect a return of the money they extort from society – the money disappears. In fact, the recipient of the money will likely spend (consume) the money on what we call consumables. This means the so-called investment does not return to the investor. It is consumed, lost to future "investment". This is not effective giving.

Compare the loss on consumables with the loss to the taxpayer who would otherwise have been able to invest his own money in a company or stock. This is not an effective "investment". Consider the billions and even trillions of dollars spent on social justice programs in our economy; this money could have been spent on creating companies, jobs, products, and wealth in an economy not burdened by effective altruism. Talk about evidence and reason.

Just this fact (of wasted money) proves that effective altruism is not effective nor moral by any means. Effective altruists claim that their virtue signaling proves their "values" are good (because it makes them *feel* good about themselves). Yet, it takes only a little math to recognize that effective altruism does not add up to *good* by any means.

The idea of "making the world a better place" is one commonly held all over the world. Although it sounds good, the idea ignores the fact that few of us are able to change the world to any substantial degree. Wanting to do good is a fine sentiment but it does not fulfill a moral mandate. The world will continue to be what it is regardless. Every person who works solely for himself is making the world a better place. Yet, it is typical of moralists to preach "duty" as the only way to be moral, which harms good people. There is plenty of evidence to suggest that self-interest is a better way to make the world a better place. Under effective altruism, making the world a better place is essentially a collectivist notion, a public relations scam that drives people into herds of self-sacrificial slaves. The concept means that altruism is the only way to be moral and that sacrifice for the collective is the only good.

Worse, the preachers of effective altruism are using altruistic human sacrifice as a weapon to entrap people and make them submit to higher taxes, pay for wars, and allow for greater and larger government programs.

The pressure that is put upon people to sacrifice to others or suffer opprobrium is a travesty. Such concepts as ESG and DEI[6] work like hatchets that decapitate people and divest them of their moral instincts and sentiments. The practice of canceling people for exhibiting traits of independence and individualism is also cruel and abusive.

There are many ways to solve human problems that do not involve ESG and DEI. Concepts like individual rights, the Bill of Rights, free market theories, and capitalism provide great arguments for solving human problems that most progressives consider to be evil. This is because of their need to eliminate political opposition and their willingness to criminalize dissent and speech while putting political opposition in prison.

Hence, the contributions made by effective altruists to mostly Democratic politicians was seen as advancing effective altruism, because the Democrats could not only protect Fried's FTX against regulators, but also make them look like good guys trying to do the most good. That's one way to win elections – PR the Republicans into

---

[6] Equity, Social, and Government and Diversity, Equity, and Inclusion

oblivion using effective altruism as the motive. Yet, it is clear that any concept requiring the disenfranchisement of dissent and opposition cannot make the world a better place. For that, see George Soros.

Effective altruism is a biased view that preaches cause neutrality (cause and effect) and claims to avoid confirmation bias[7]. In fact, the concept of altruism violates the principle of cause and effect and is full of confirmation bias. In fact, effective altruists are oblivious to the damage they do to people caught in their web, and especially, they refuse to criticize themselves on a foundation of reason. They do not recognize the fact that altruism violates the human mind and denies how man survives (by the use of the mind). Additionally, they expose their bias that the individual deserves to be exploited by their various schemes (ESG, DEI, CRT). This bias is confirmed by their gender politics, identity politics, and anti-capitalism. Their enemies, white people, certain collectives (such as Asians and Jewish people), rich people, and capitalists are

---

[7] Confirmation bias is a cognitive bias that leads people to seek, interpret, and remember information that confirms their existing beliefs or values. It is a common psychological phenomenon that affects how people process and analyze information. Confirmation bias can influence people's decisions and judgments, and make them resistant to change their opinions even when faced with contradictory evidence. Source: https://www.dictionary.com/browse/confirmation-bias

found everywhere in society suffering without a peep of defense by the media.

One tactic that effective altruists use is the tactic of guilting people in order to "trap" them into positions they might not otherwise accept. This is why you see people eagerly accept the notion of sacrifice for the group. They are too afraid of being considered selfish for thinking of themselves. This tactic, and the numerous attacks on dissenters, are cruel and abusive; they are the use of moral force to manipulate people and keep them from challenging or straying from altruism. This tactic of moral insinuation takes place all over society, in government, in the courts, in education, in movies and other forms of manipulation.

Finally, consider this: communism promised a new socialist man who would finally make communism into a successful utopian end. Over time, the idea of social engineering developed to advance the communist and socialist causes. The communist philosophy mercilessly criticized "selfish" business people and sought to educate children to accept the "value" of self-sacrifice. They also sought to use lies to "nudge" adults to enable government coercion. Don't be surprised then that effective altruists are likewise seeking to create the new socialist man by the same nefarious means. They seek to portray themselves as efficient planners of society. They are the do-gooders, the technocrats who "know" what society needs: more sacrifice. To hide the original altruist intent, they seek to portray themselves as pragmatists who know what society needs. Yet, like virtually all pragmatists, they fail to accomplish their ends because there is no connection between altruism and reality.

To understand why the original sources of altruism do not work, we can recall ancient rituals of human sacrifice. Modern altruism is a metaphor for the ancient human sacrificial rite. First, leaders of society train human minds to accept a contradiction; the contradiction that you can accomplish a good result by doing damage to a scapegoat. The killing of the scapegoat is an act of sacrifice; it gives the illusion that the scapegoat is willingly giving up his life for the sake of the collective. They even turned human sacrifice into a sacred act of obedience to God who supposedly loved human sacrifice.

Once the scapegoat is killed something magical is supposed to happen. The sacrifice is supposed to save the world. Yet, any rational human being knows that there is no tangible connection between the act of killing a scapegoat and the expectation that something good will happen. It is a non sequitur to expect magical results from the act of killing (sacrificing) an individual. This applies equally to the altruistic notion that something magical happens when we tax productive people. Nothing beneficial results from this act.

Let us examine the act of killing a human being done by a criminal. The goal of the criminal is to remove the killed person from life. Either the killer wants something from the victim, or he thinks that the removal of this person will accomplish something good. As we can see, no good can be created by killing a normal productive person. Likewise, the act of killing a scapegoat in the rite of human sacrifice does no good in the real world, and this fact applies to altruism which is a taking of life and values. Consider the import of this wicked idea that killing someone, or taking his values, is a beneficent idea. The conceptual connection between ancient sacrificial rites and effective altruism is clear – they are the same thing, and they accomplish nothing good. We have to wonder why intelligent people would consider human sacrifice to be good. Yet, centuries of human development have been sabotaged by altruism.

Of course, the only outcome of ritual of human sacrifice is the killing of one individual for the sake of collective results that do not come about. Killing one individual does not save a collective – it only kills the individual. Likewise for all forms of human sacrifice and altruism.

We can ascertain this truth by recognizing that human sacrifice is perennially practiced with no beneficial result – otherwise, we would not be constantly repeating the ritual. In other words, sacrifice is being constantly repeated because it didn't work the last time.

Why haven't people noticed this? Because they have no sense of cause and effect. Their expectation of benefit through sacrifice is still-born, and no one has noticed that if altruism does not work, it is fruitless. Altruism is a scam that results in mass murder. It kills a scapegoat and attains no beneficial result. It only attains the death of the scapegoat. Altruism is an ineffectual death trap.

What is effective altruism? It is the promise to make things better by confiscating value from productive scapegoats. It is the promise of a better world by making the world worse.

Understanding How Altruism Works

To better understand how altruism (including effective altruism) works, I would like to offer a visual demonstration. First, we will focus on the individual because, in my view, altruism, throughout history, has been about "looting" the individual of his values or life.

First, we start with the human being and his/her tools of survival.

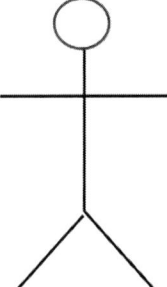

Human being

Means of survival: exceptional mind, conceptual capacity, logical reasoning, induction, knowledge, value development and value creation.

Resources: Senses, hearing, sight, touch, smell, taste.

Secondly, we move to the work the human being does to create value.

He/she educates the mind and works on material reality to create values.

The mind is man's critical tool for survival. In modern society, it is thought that the mind must be free to function if man and society are to be affluent and successful.

Thirdly, we see his storage of his created values in a metaphorical "back pack". Most values are traded for common stores of value in currency and coins.

"Ayn Rand defined value as that which one acts to gain and/or keep. A value is an object of action. In this sense we can say that everyone pursues values. This includes any goal-directed behavior."[8]

Values are the key to human behavior and the reason the individual seeks knowledge and skills.

---

[8] http://rebirthofreason.com/Articles/Younkins/Ayn_Rands_Value_Theory.shtml#:~:text=Ayn%20Rand%20defined%20value%20as%20that%20which%20one,is%20observable.%20We%20see%20people%20going%20after%20things.

The enemy of value is the man who would demand them in the name of altruistic giving. This includes criminals, politicians, preachers, and college professors of the leftist variety.

Fourthly, the demand that the individual give up values as a matter of morality will be made while the individual is taught that he has no choice. He will suffer guilt and diminishment if he does not sacrifice. The soft cry of altruism is now his constant companion. He fears others – all others.[9]

The altruist re-distributor preaches about the importance of living for others. He demands that the producer of values give them up for others. Or else.

Fifthly, we see the re-distributor directing the productive individual to give up his values to the "victim" whose sign says, "Help Me!".

---

[9] See my book, "Finding your Soft Cry" https://amzn.to/46lA1tf

Moral pronouncements from authorities demand sacrifice for the person who was "supposed" to give his life and values for others.

Sixthly, we see all three of these individuals. The sacrificer has very little of his values left, is tired and ready to expire. The re-distributor has a very full back pack while the victim has received very little.

The re-distributor is wealthy. The productive individual does not have a right to the values he has created and the downtrodden is still poor. The incentive for the creator of values declines and he begins to diminish his output because he knows anything he creates will be taken away.

With little output of values there is little input and poverty begins to take over.

Seventhly, we see the result. The sacrificer is dead from poverty and starvation, the re-distributor is dead, and the victim is dead as well. They have all starved to death because no one is producing enough values. This is because altruism is a false promise of better days ahead. In fact, the sacrificer has no incentive to create values, the re-distributor is not able to create values, and the so-called downtrodden is also not able to create values.

Altruism is a death trap.

There are few critics of altruism today because most people focus on the supposed benefits to the downtrodden that altruism is supposed to produce. The fact that such people seldom benefit in the long-term is overlooked on the moral steamroller created by people who claim to represent the "good" brought about by altruism.

In fact, the damage done to the value producer is overlooked. Yet, in reality, no amount of semantics will make that damage go away which exposes the LIE that altruism does no harm to the producer; but makes him a better person. Yet, it is this damage that makes altruism evil and destructive in general. Social systems that demand sacrifice, such as communism, socialism, and welfare statism are replete with damage to the productive individual and society as a whole. Altruism is evil because people are forced by it into slavery and poverty. They are submissive to a level of control that is engaged in primarily by both leftist and rightist altruists. Effective altruism is only effective in this sense: for centuries all forms of altruism have devastated society and their proponents have gotten away with their LIES about doing good for mankind in general.

Altruism destroys the human mind and the ability of men to live fruitfully and productively.

There never seems to be a shortage of people who need help; and of people who have been trained since childhood to help them. Many people suppress their "need" to live their lives to the highest of their abilities and in pursuit of their singular happiness. When the call to sacrifice comes, too many are eager to escape the process of self-love and descend into the habit of "helping others" – the call to sacrifice becomes the call to signal virtuous intent – without a true understanding of what is true virtue.

Altruism is a philosophy that holds all people to be more important than the individual. Altruism requires an attack on the individual, an attempt to steal the values the individual creates. Altruists feel they must attack intelligence and portray it as oppressive, and this creates fear of others in the victim. These attacks, however, are oppressive in themselves. They declare intelligence to be an affront to the average person and, in some circumstances, the effective altruist must portray himself as "a man of the people", as a lover of humanity, in order to avoid being accused of having overwhelming hatred of intelligence and the "violence" that comes with it through expropriation of value.

As a young person, very young, I was confronted by the moral police. I had been playing with a toy that I had brought to school. This toy was a 5-cent plastic car whose wheels were also plastic. It was a simple tool given to me by my father and I was fascinated with it to the point of bringing it to school. By all standards, the toy was very small, but it was mine. As I was playing with it, another larger boy came over to me and picked it up so he could play with it.

According to the moral police, there is something you are not supposed to do if you are a moral little boy; and that is make another boy cry because you have asserted your rights. This was the lesson I took from this. I learned that my initial outrage was wrong in some way and that I should have let the boy play with my toy and considered THAT to be a moral act. I was wrong to be "selfish" and this was unacceptable to the moral police. Finally, the teacher gave me a lecture about how I owed other people good actions (and I assumed that I did not deserve those action from them). She told me that I should report to her at the end of the school day what I had done that day for others.

Needless to say, I ditched that instruction, and she never asked me about it in the future. Still, this incident illustrates the dangerous aspects of altruism and how they harm young people that have it imposed upon them.

But this is not the history of altruism we have come to know. Most people have been indoctrinated into the idea that altruism is a highly beneficent concept that has done tremendous good in the world. When people hear that someone has sacrificed for others, one is told about the tremendous benefits that came to the people who were served. In fact, this is all talk; there is very little benefit to the downtrodden, but a great deal of prestige for the sacrificer, awards (largely self-generated), and laundered money.

We seldom hear about the other side of altruism, and that is the side that measures the losses to the people who have been exploited and robbed of their values. Many of the sacrificed people have lost significant values over their life, and, because they have been indoctrinated to focus only on the "good" being done for others, they seldom learn to count their own losses especially in the area of the intellectual parasitism imposed upon them. Those people who represent altruism as a benign and beneficial concept most often assume that only good can come from the altruistic acts of giving. What they ignore is the fact that man cannot be "perfected" and made to be the quintessential example of utopia. History has shown that the truly perfect altruist cannot be created through more and more giving, as we have indicated through the images we posted in this chapter. Altruism is a death trap masquerading as utopia.

Additionally, we must consider the almost automatic association of altruism with God or religion. There is no reason to associate the confiscation of values or property with the will of God. Since God is a non-existent entity, the association of altruistic action (which is a "taking") with God is unnecessary and harmful to moral action. In fact, it is just as easy, morally, to associate confiscation of values with evil. Such confiscation is more akin to doing evil to honest and productive individuals.

Finally, the association of altruism with communism, socialism, and religion are each a non sequitur. It does not follow that each of these systems represent the good when, in reality, altruism has nothing to do with good when you consider the historical consequences of such concepts. Communism is associated with the confiscation of values away from honest people and self-interested men (through the destruction of people in genocidal acts). Socialism is likewise associated with the evil taking of values by means of literal enslavement, while the sacrificial pyre of religion is equally evil when we consider that the individual has every right to keep what he has earned, and should be able to do so without guilt. Altruism is not about good versus evil or light versus dark. It is literally about the evil of taking values from good people and destroying those people in the process. Altruism is evil masquerading as good. It is about gaslighting people into thinking that they, as individuals, are evil if they do not accept the falsity of altruistic taking.

Altruism is also not about love. On the contrary, altruism is about "taking" in the name of "giving". Altruists must gaslight people into believing that altruism has the ability to help people.

Gaslighting is the practice of one person making another person question his or her own mind or version of reality. Gaslighting involves seemingly changing the reality in the mind of another in order to engender sacrifice of the mind while creating emergencies (lies) that require concerted action.

Making people doubt the reality of their own observations, knowledge, ownership, and self-interest, because they have been taught that college educated politicians and CEOs (the gas lighters), know what is best for them.

The gas lighter tells the gas lighted: "You don't have a right to feel that way. You must feel the way I tell you. You don't understand your feelings or thoughts. You should think what I tell you."

Deflection is the gas lighter's tactic of changing the subject constantly (or blaming the gas lighted person for having bad motives) as if the original thought is wrong. The gas lighted individual, if he has no self-confidence about his thinking, becomes the hapless victim of evil men intent on ruling society (or the lives of individuals). You see this every day in the media.

Denying the individual's reality by insisting to him that something that didn't happen happened is metaphysical gaslighting. This is the culmination of the pragmatist goal of making men into confused slaves.

The opposite of altruism is individualism. Individualism is about self-sufficiency and living independently. This means the individual should never be penalized for his productive activities and that individual rights mean living for the goodness found in the self. It is the opposite of the concept of "service" which is connected to the demand that the individual should be required to serve others over living for him- or herself. This idea of service is the way that altruists rope individuals into living lives that put others first rather than the self.

In fact, the idea of service to others seems benign enough until the individual realizes, toward the end, that through all his life, he had been duped into a life of servitude and that this very concept that had caused many and various psychological problems. He had never known that serving others had deprived him of happiness.

Psychological depressions were created by the idea that putting others first was the very cause of anxiety (fear of others) and unhappiness (ignoring his own interests over many years).

The proper individual learns, over time, that he should be seeking more ways to live for himself rather than to compartmentalize his life through limiting sacrificial acts. This compartmentalization of morality divides moral goals into an altruist perspective. On the other hand, a selfish perspective creates a moral conflict (with society) that is difficult to live with. It leads, primarily to what Ayn Rand called the "anti-conceptual mentality".

To understand this further, we need to look at the examples of countless people who, generally, live conflicted lives because they are never able to reconcile the differences between self-sacrifice and self-interest. As semi-altruistic givers of their values, they lose those values and suffer from a sort of value deprivation, and as semi-selfish individuals, they feel a sense of knowing that they will never be able to fully live and love their selves. As altruists, they believe that they should sacrifice for others at all times, and as semi-selfish individuals they feel guilty for having a sense of love-of-self and strive to avoid loving themselves especially when it is needed and deserved.

Understanding How Selfish Living Works

When I use the word "selfish living", I am not referring to the kind of living that intentionally hurts others and steals values from them. I am referring to thinking of your own interest first without regard to the negative opinions or moral codes of others. It is not a "me first" attitude but a benign "ME FIRST" attitude that seeks to identify the values that will benefit your life first. It means making competent decisions about your long-term values and how you will pursue them.

The choice to survive through self-interested action is part of the functioning of the human mind. Survival requires intellectual certainty and effective action. If you look at the images in the above chapter "Understanding How Altruism Works", you can see that the reverse of altruism is effective selfishness – and that there is no such thing as effective altruism.

This time, we start with the human being and his/her tools of survival. As we said, intellectual certainty leads to selfish action.

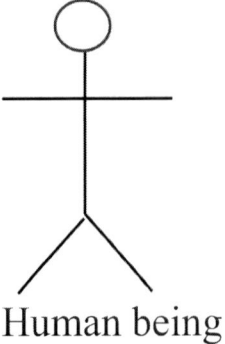
Human being

Means of survival: exceptional mind, conceptual capacity, logical reasoning, induction, knowledge, value development and value creation. Resources: Senses, hearing, sight, touch, smell, taste.

How does human morality happen? Again, we move to the work the human being does to create value, the work of survival.

He/she educates the mind and body while working on material reality to create values.

The mind is man's critical tool for survival. In modern society, we learn that the mind must be free to function if man is to be affluent and successful. This means a repudiation of the concepts of sacrifice and collectivism. A free man is a successful man.

We learn this by comparing the survival status of the productive individual with the survival status of the unproductive individual.

Here, we see the productive person's storage of created values in the same metaphorical "back pack" as above.

Here we see again that values are the key motivators for human behavior and the reason why the moral individual seeks knowledge and skills. The enemy of value is the man who would demand values be given to him in the name of altruistic giving. "Help Me", he says.

By comparing self-sufficiency and dependency we can see that self-sufficiency represents all that is good in life while dependency represents the zero. This means that the human mind can only bring life if it is allowed to think for itself. Invariably, the morally free individual is self-sufficient and feels responsible for his or her own production. This leads us to material products and their beneficent influence on life. Altruism, on the other hand, limits free minds by stifling production which leads to exploitation of productive people. This eventually destroys the incentive to produce, limits action, creates loss, and causes intellectual corruption.

Self-sufficiency requires the development of intellectual activity and intellectual property rights.

When the individual is allowed to retain the values created, he or she develops a surplus of value which enables more investment that grows and grows. This surplus enables more jobs for others willing to work.

Overall, survival becomes easier because of the cumulative impact of the investment of surplus production. Even the poor, in this case, are given a tremendous boost in their survival as society becomes more and more affluent.

Notice that, at this point, the negative influence of altruism is eliminated and there can only be good results for all people involved. Without altruism influencing his decisions, the unproductive individual becomes incentivized to produce, and his meager efforts can still produce enough for bare subsistence. Knowing that he has no claim on the work of others helps him discover the value of work.

Kantianism, Menticide, and Altruism

> "...it may be presumed that men will be ready to believe what they wish to believe, and that no hoax will be too preposterous to be without a following" – Prof. Francis Kelsey University of Michigan 1911

Altruism and other related concepts such as collectivism, dictatorship, authoritarianism, and totalitarianism require a systematic and intentional undermining of the individual's conscious mind. The primitive form of mind murder, menticide, is the demand for a fully empty mind. The leaders of society believe it is easier to advance their social goals when men cannot challenge their authority. When men cannot resist the calls for altruism and human sacrifice, when they cannot challenge bad ideas, they cannot intelligently resist authorities. By murdering the minds of individuals, leaders attain the freedom to compel people to do what they want.

An empty mind is a fearful mind. It functions within a vacuum of empty silence. Although it has many disconnected knowledge units, many of its ideas come from the intrusions of teachers telling lies.

Most of us have had our minds murdered by teachers. Theirs is the art of menticide, the result of thousands of destructive words that came from modern philosophy. Kant's philosophy is responsible for the large-scale murder of the mind. It is this philosophy that rescued religion and human sacrifice as moral principles.

To eliminate the scrouge of altruism, we must learn to understand Kant's virulent philosophy and remove it as a human institution. We must learn how Kant destroyed the minds of modern men and began the process of exposing the evil that has infested, not only the human animal, but civilization as a whole. To kill the humanity in man, the thieves of society must first murder the human mind.

How did Kant succeed in murdering the human mind? First, he invented two opposite principles, one, called analytic, and the second synthetic. Dr. Peikoff explains it: An analytic truth: "can be validated *merely by an analysis of the meaning of its constituent concepts* (thus these are called analytic truths)."[10]

Peikoff continues: "If one merely specifies the definitions of the relevant concepts in any of (analytic) propositions, and then applies the laws directly, and that to deny it would be to endorse a logical contradiction. Hence, these are also called

---

[10] Introduction to Objectivist Epistemology by Ayn Rand, Softcover, Meridian

"logical truths," meaning that they can be validated merely by correctly applying the laws of logic."

Also, "Analytic truths represent concrete instances of the Law of Identity; as such, they are also frequently called "Tautologies" (which, etymologically, means that the proposition repeats "the same thing"; e.g., "A rational animal is a rational animal," "The solid form of water is a solid"). Since all of the propositions of logic and mathematics can ultimately be analyzed and validated in this fashion, these two subjects, it is claimed, fall entirely within the "analytic" or "tautological" half of human knowledge." An analytic truth has the distinction of being connected to reality only by means of its definition which means that it is not connected to reality at all. Even the fact that the definition might use a conceptual truth does not ensure that an analytic truth is connected to reality in any way.

What does it mean to say that a particular analytic proposition is an analytic truth? Keep in mind, they are not saying the analytic proposition is the truth, they are saying it is an "analytic" truth. In fact, a proposition that is said to be analytic only means that it is a tautology; it does not mean that it is true.

So, is half of human knowledge made up of analytic truths that are merely tautological, and, to take it further, such a "truth" can make no claim that it represents knowledge of reality. Analytic truths are nothing more than definitions of definitions – words disconnected from reality. They are the first step to menticide.

The rest of human knowledge is made up of what are called "synthetic" truths. Peikoff goes on to define a synthetic truth:

"*Synthetic* propositions, on the other hand ... by most of the statements of daily life and of the sciences—are said to be entirely different on all these counts. A "synthetic" proposition is defined as one which *cannot* be validated merely by an analysis of the meanings of definitions of its constituent concepts. For instance, conceptual or definitional analysis alone, it is claimed, could not tell one whether ice floats on water, or what volume of liquid results when various quantities of water and ethyl alcohol are mixed.

"In this type of case, said Kant, the predicate of the proposition (e.g., "floats on water") states something about the subject ("ice") which is not already contained in the meaning of the subject-concept. (The proposition represents a *synthesis* of the subject with a new predicate, hence the name.) Such truths cannot be validated merely by correctly applying the laws of logic; they do not represent concrete instances of the Law of Identity. To deny such truths is to maintain *a falsehood*, but *not a self-contradiction*. Thus, it is false to assert that "a man has three eyes," or that "Ice sinks in water"—but, it is the *facts* of the case, not the laws of logic, which condemn such statements. Accordingly, synthetic truths are held to be 'factual' as opposed to "logical" or "tautological" in character."[11]

Kant has created a set of dual concepts, neither of which enable cognition and truth. An "analytic truth" is tied to a definition rather than to reality, while a synthetic truth breaks the connection between the definition (analytic) and other characteristics of a concept. Both concepts break the connection to cognitive efficacy by creating a split between two anti-concepts. The "analytic-synthetic dichotomy" represents the development of 1) approximate concepts and 2) subjective concepts. The result of separating the mind from reality is menticide.

Concepts that separate the mind from reality are properly called anti-concepts. Ayn Rand writes, "An anti-concept is an unnecessary and rationally unusable term designed to replace and obliterate some legitimate concept. The use of anti-concepts gives the listeners a sense of approximate understanding. But in the realm of cognition, nothing is as bad as the approximate . . ."[12]

In my view, an "analytic truth" is an anti-concept designed to replace the real term "a truth" (that

---

[11] Ibid
[12] The Ayn Rand Letter, Credibility and Polarization by Ayn Rand

merely describes a logical proposition in dialectic form). A tautology can refer to reality, but, properly, it must be validated by an examination (an induction) that connects the words of a proposition to reality. An analytic truth refers only to the word without a connection of that word to something real. A tautology is nothing more than a floating abstraction disconnected from a grounding that can only be found in reality.

In effect, an "analytic truth" represents an effort to turn an epistemological principle into an approximate metaphysical one. Who has the ability to define analytic truths? Who can teach us how to do this and what gives these people the knowledge necessary for such definitions of words?

Likewise, the term "synthetic truth" is an anti-concept for cognitive truth that obscures the difference between real, usable knowledge and subjective, collective knowledge.

Both terms, analytic and synthetic, destroy objective truth, because they obscure the meaning of the law of identity and its connection to reality. For instance, the term "analytic truths" suggests that such terms are "necessary". It implies that they hold true for all times, despite the fact that they are constantly changing and cannot refer to reality in any sense. It describes only words, and their meanings, they tell us, (rationalistically) are not necessary but contingent. How can anything in reality be contingent? And that's the point: contingency is not in reality – it is in the rationalistic words used. It is a form of nominalism.

In the practical sense, the integration of the analytic with the subjective collective consciousness is constantly switching. Finally, the analytic (which Kant calls *a priori* knowledge) destroys understanding while the synthetic (which he calls *a posteriori*) refers only to the integration of *a priori* knowledge with *a posteriori* terms. Yet, we aren't finished with Kant's philosophy. As we have seen, Kant has tried to use anti-concepts to turn his epistemology (analytic-synthetic dichotomy) into a metaphysical principle, to confuse all thinking, and he also pulls out of the ether another split called the noumenal versus phenomenal realms of reality.

"According to Kant, it is vital always to distinguish between the distinct realms of phenomena and noumena. Phenomena are the appearances, which constitute our experience; noumena are the (presumed) things themselves, which constitute reality. All of our synthetic a priori judgments apply only to the phenomenal realm, not the noumenal. (It is only at this level, with respect to what we can experience, that we are justified in imposing the structure of our concepts onto the objects of our knowledge.)

Since the thing in itself (Ding an sich) would by definition be entirely independent of our experience of it, we are utterly ignorant of the noumenal realm.

"Thus, on Kant's view, the most fundamental laws of nature, like the truths of mathematics, are knowable precisely because they make no effort to describe the world as it really is but rather prescribe the structure of the world as we experience it. By applying the pure forms of sensible intuition and the pure concepts of the understanding, we achieve a systematic view of the phenomenal realm but learn nothing of the noumenal realm. Math and science are certainly true of the phenomena; only metaphysics claims to instruct us about the noumena."[13]

Of course, the first question to ask of Kant is "how did he know these truths?" What evidence did he provide that validates his view of the noumenal and phenomenal realms? What is a "realm" in Kant's view?

Scholars will inform us that Kant's "realms" are made up of knowledge in both the noumenal and phenomenal contexts. For instance:

"Immanuel Kant is a famous philosopher who divided the realms of knowledge into two realms; the phenomenal realm and the noumenal realm. The phenomenal realm represents the world as it

---

[13] http://www.philosophypages.com/hy/5g.htm

is perceived and the noumenal realm represents the world as it really is independent of perception. This is a fantastic division because it realizes that what we perceive is not always fully accurate."[14] My point is that if we are talking about knowledge in both the phenomenal and noumenal realms, we are limited by Kant to the internal workings of the mind. There is nothing to connect Kant's realms with the real world. If the phenomenal realm is the world as it is perceived, anything that is perceived cannot be real. There is no way to accommodate the view that the phenomenal realm represents anything at all. How is it possible to fully understand a realm that exists in the mind but has no connection to the "perceived". Recall the various statements made in debate where one debater excoriates the other for presenting views as he perceives them. "Oh, so that is your perception. How can you trust your perceptions when they exist only in your mind?" On the other hand, the phenomenal realm is supposed to be human knowledge (in the mind) that represents the world as it exists independently of the mind. How is that possible? How can we have human knowledge in the mind while it also exists independently of the mind. The

---

[14] https://finntronaut.wordpress.com/2020/11/06/the-phenomenal-and-the-noumenal-realm/#:~:text=Immanuel%20Kant%20is%20a%20famous%20philosopher%20who%20divided,world%20as%20it%20really%20is%20independent%20of%20perception.

contradiction here is palpable. Yet, for 300 (or so) years men have been accepting these notions. How does Kant deal with these contradictions? It is really hard to say. Having reduced "reality" to mere perceptions, on the one hand, and to products of the mind on the other hand, we are left in the lurch trying to understand this. The answer is that Kant invents a new concept called the "intuition" in order to bridge the gap between the realm that man's mind creates and the realm that he merely perceives.

After capturing the mind in the phenomenal and noumenal realms, Kant escapes his incongruity thusly:

"...In the Transcendental Aesthetic of the first Critique, Kant writes: "In whatever way and through whatever means a cognition may (be) related to objects, that through which it relates immediately to them, and at which all thought as a means is directed as an end, is intuition. This, however, takes place only insofar as the object is given to us; but this in turn, is possible only if it affects the mind in a certain way. This capacity...to acquire representations...is called sensibility. Objects are therefore given to us by means of sensibility, and it alone affords us intuitions..." (A 19/B 33).

"Here's a start at understanding Kant's conception of intuition: intuitions are representations, given in sensation, that provide the material--the starting point--for all cognition."[15]

For Kant, it appears, "intuition" provides the "synthesis" that connects objects to cognition. Imagine what happens in the human mind here: An individual that wants to understand must appeal to his intuition in order to attain cognitive clarity. If this isn't mysticism, I don't know what is.

Since morality is an outgrowth of metaphysics and epistemology, we can now examine how Kant committed his menticide. By firstly, invalidating human knowledge, he declares that the only way for man to attain cognition, is through "intuition". This clears the slate and places human cognition squarely on the idea that man "subjectively" creates reality by means of "pure reason" that he renames and misidentifies. Needless to say, rationalism, sensualism, and nominalism help create anti-concepts to influence morality around the idea of "duty".

At some point in life, you must come to grips with the ideas that kill your mind, and decide if you deserve it. You must, at this point realize that the killing of your mind, as done by Kant, skepticism, and the anti-mind philosophy, is in fact, the destruction of your ego, your love of self and your inability to live and achieve happiness. You can

---

[15] https://www.askphilosophers.org/question/204

choose to ignore the criticisms of altruism, or succumb to their influence and let guilt rule your life, or you can fight for your mind, for certainty, and for your ego that is the core of your being. Refuse to give in to the attempted murder of your mind and ego.

Altruism and Agoraphobia

Agoraphobia is an anxiety disorder developed by a fear of open spaces such as marketplaces, public squares, and crowded places from which escape seems difficult. Generally, it is a fear of other people and the places where they congregate.

As such, the fear engendered by agoraphobia is psychological in nature. This means it is sourced in irrational thinking rather than reason. Yet, I argue, people are taught to fear others by our educational systems, that suggests agoraphobia is caused by altruism and the fear of the irrational social demands of collective self-sacrifice.

The real-life consequences of agoraphobia are certainly catastrophic for the individual. When an individual is constantly beset with the demands of others to sacrifice, the psychological consequence is that he has no choice but to obey. This is the power of altruism: The constant imposition of it has the subconscious effect of making people fear moral judgment even for normal self-interested actions.

Agoraphobia has devastating consequences for human happiness. I believe it creates tremendous levels of physical tension and anxiety which threaten human peace of mind and happiness. In a very real sense, human psychology has failed to identify this psychological syndrome and its consequences for human life. So much tension is developed by this thought process of worrying what people think that it makes many people vulnerable to gaslighting and manipulation by the practitioners of altruism and human sacrifice.

Agoraphobia is likewise such a powerful negative motivator because virtually everyone believes that the idea of sacrifice is to be obeyed without question. This power affects the innocent person more than it affects the so-called narcissistic person who is mostly impervious to attempts at moral conditioning. Altruism is, in essence, an effort to block moral action in the name of moral action which is what makes it such a sinister moral factor that few understand. It is, at base, the cause of immorality in the name of morality, of injustice in the name of justice. The individual is forced to "swear an oath" that he will always and instinctively work for the sake of others regardless of whether it negatively affects his life and actions. This is a deadly trap brought on by the fear of others.

How do Dictatorships use Altruism to kill People?

Few people know about the perennial use of altruism to advance the goals of dictatorship. Leaders conspiring for power routinely invoke the need of "the people" to sacrifice for the sake of the "whole". Still, today, most people do not know that altruism is a means for installing communism, socialism, and fascism, all of which use this moral philosophy to justify their expropriations of the peoples' product.

One of the deadliest deceptions of altruism is its use as justification for genocide and other forms of mass murder. Genocide is the mass murder, usually of millions of people, for the sake of getting rid of political opposition. Dictators think they must eliminate political enemies who prosper in society and know the difference between freedom and slavery.

The cloud of deception over the value of altruism is the idea that helping people is somehow good. Yet altruism is not about helping people as we saw this in the chapter "Understanding How Altruism Works". Dictatorships routinely use the demand for sacrifice to compel citizens to act in ways that harm them. People are often coerced through high taxes, group indoctrination meetings, speeches, media, education, and written communications to see their roles in society as sacrificial victims.

How does death become a feature of altruism and genocide? There are four examples of nations that have used altruism to justify mass murder. First, the Nazis of Germany started with racism, in particular antisemitism, in order to destroy millions of Jews. Jews were wrongly considered exploiters and thieves who should be eliminated. What few people notice about Nazi hatred is that Jews generally were educated, prosperous, and affluent people who should be destroyed according to the hateful Nazis. The Germans saw the Jewish people among them as the cause for many of their woes before, during, and after the first World War.

The willingness of the Nazis to kill Jews is not beyond what other nations did to affluent people. The Soviets, on the other hand, persecuted affluent people who had owned businesses during pre-revolutionary times. These persecuted groups were called "bourgeoise" who had their properties confiscated by and outlawed from labor unions. The Soviets also punished Jews and a separate group called the Kulaks who were also affluent and independent.

The Chinese also persecuted affluent shop owners while unleashing terror on these people and destroying property. This was called the Red Purge and included the persecution of intellectuals and educators who were critical of communism.

Finally, the communists in Cambodia persecuted millions of educators and intellectuals strictly because they were critical of Pol Pot and other communists. Pol Pot even killed people who wore glasses solely because they might be considered too intelligent.

These genocidal policies were all justified by the hatred communists felt toward anyone who sought to be successful in society, meaning they saw their political opposition to be made up of people who fostered individualism, egoism, and individual rights. All of these "types" of people were considered to be unwilling to sacrifice for the glory of the state. They were, therefore, enemies of the state who had to be eradicated so society could advance to the completely self-sacrificing utopian society.

How Altruism and Guilt Cancel People

In another book, I wrote: "When people are confronted by the imposition of bad ideas, they become deluded and confused. It is only people in this condition who are susceptible to the machinations of administrators and politicians. Both modern philosophy and religion have their own means of causing delusions in the minds of men; and a true solution can only come through a complete "cleaning of the slate" accompanied by a new quest for reason.

"It is worth noting that both left and right admonish men for being selfish – and it is this attack that deludes men into thinking they might be living an evil life unless they give up their selfishness and devote their lives to others. Through admonishments of this type, through attacks on selfishness, both left and right impose mass psychosis on humanity. Men become consumed with a need to give up their values for others and this likewise consumes their minds in a struggle for a form of redemption that consumes all of their actions. (Slightly edited content)

"Note that, in this regard, the one thing most modern thinkers do not reject (when they reject religion) is collectivism and altruism. The result is secular altruism and mysticism that makes men into virtual slaves." (What this means is that the two false premises of altruism and mysticism continue to destroy men's lives as modern thinkers. These two ideas go without challenge and continue to dominate the minds of men – which resulted in the victory of dictatorship that is built upon these ideas.) (Parenthesis is added content)

Examples of how altruism is used to cancel people are numerous:
- Anti-capitalism, wherever we find it, is replete with attacks on self-interest, egoism, and the profit motive. The basis of all these attacks is that capitalism is pro-ego, pro-self-interest, pro-profit, etc., none of which are bad by any means. This anti-capitalism comes from the charges of religion and modern Marxism, both of which denigrated merchants, money lenders, and capitalists as evil exploiters and thieves guided by self-interest. Ignoring the genocide of socialism and communism, anti-capitalists attempt to whitewash the murderous nature of altruism in an attempt to corrupt the minds of men into accepting genocidal murder and ritualized human sacrifice as normal.
- Religion is also anti-ego. The idea of sacrificing the life of Jesus, in particular, was considered a monumental and historic sacrifice for the collective. Religion

excoriates individuals who proclaim a dedication to their own success and admonishes men for such pursuits, encouraging them to deny all pursuits that benefit their lives. The sacrifice of Jesus was a call to sacrifice by all men. It views self-interest as a double evil and sacrifice for others as a double good. To deny the value of Jesus' sacrifice is to doom men to destruction in Hell.

- Environmentalism, in particular, is based upon the dissipation (through indoctrination) of human energy and affluent living. As a Marxist movement, environmentalism seeks to educate people into the "belief" that man's actions (using fossil fuels) will create the apocalypse. This requires the belief that men are evil and avaricious by nature, so the altruists must paint the results of man's actions in such a way that we must be afraid of disasters that will come if man is allowed to be economically and morally free. If we are sufficiently afraid of ourselves and what we do for our survival, then we can be steamrolled into destroying industrial progress. This is all justified by the notion that man is, by nature, selfish and evil and that, properly, he must sacrifice (altruistically) by dissipating his production of energy and other useful products, all of which give man a better life. The environmentalists are, in effect, akin to religious bigots with a hatred for man and freedom.[16]

- Globalism is one of the biggest "conspiracies" of all. Globalists are also Marxists who seek to turn all men into willing slaves. By denigrating capitalism, and offering themselves up as "competent" technocrats, they teach people to hate self-interest and encourage them to turn their actions against "capitalists" that they blindly believe are intent on enslaving people.
- Covid mandates are intended to confiscate the machines and medical cures that save peoples' lives. The altruists among the globalists seek to deny effective medical cures to the people and replace them with genocidal murder through nationalized medical care physicians. Such mandates require human sacrifice and turn sick people

---

[16] Quote: "…the mainstream knowledge system we rely on to help us evaluate what to do about the crucial issue of fossil fuels—the system that is telling us that the "experts" say we must rapidly eliminate fossil fuel use—cannot be trusted because it is operating on the anti-human, anti-energy, anti-impact framework.

"To know what to do about the crucial issue of fossil fuels, we need a full-context evaluation of continuing fossil fuel use—its full benefits and side-effects—that synthesizes the best expert research using the human flourishing framework, including the goal of advancing human flourishing (not eliminating human impact) and the "wild potential" of Earth (not the "delicate nurturer" view)." Source "Fossil Future" by Alex Epstein https://amzn.to/461Cb0J Page 109

into global slaves whose bodies are sent to the killing fields.

Why Altruism Doesn't Work and Why it Always Fails

Altruism, as the basis of both left and right, always fails. Altruism is also the reason for the failures of socialism, communism, and fascism. The simple argument against these "isms" (that they eventually impoverish productive citizens) gives the lie to the idea that altruism produces a good result. Notice that I did not say altruism re-distributes to the poor. This is because altruism is intended to re-disdistribute funds primarily to the unproductive rich, to the leadership of the churches, the thieving politicians, and the unproductive heirs of the uber rich.

On a broader scale, altruism fails because the people who effectuate it are, themselves, dismal failures seeking to profit from the work of others. Certainly, many of them have been taught the primitive "crime" of stealing money – and for this, in modern times, they advocate leftist policies and altruistic schemes. Their inability to produce effective social institutions means they are constantly trying to overcome their lack of efficacy, which turns them into administrator types, religious types, technocrats, and failures incapable of creating positive outcomes.

The next reason that altruism fails is altruism itself. I have written about this in several books; and simply put, altruism fails because it takes the profits of some while ignoring the harmful result of the taking. Altruism is offered as the solution to moral and social problems, and, as such, it esteems theft as good when, in fact, it ruins the lives of good people who submit to it.

The next reason it fails is because altruism, as a moral philosophy, sees men as evil, incompetent, and destructive of the world. Cognitively, this sees men wrongly and results in their offering ineffective ideas that always miss their mark, ideas that do not work. They argue, wrongly, that men must accept these negative views about man because of their unearned moral authority. This last is also a cognitive mistake made by virtually all men in society. In fact, altruists have no desire to reward the poor because they regard them as dupes who can easily be scammed into voting for them. Once they attain their funds, on this basis, they only use the "unrelieved" poor to vote for them the next time. This anti-man and anti-ego perspective has disastrous consequences for the world and mankind in general.

After centuries of religious control, altruism continued to hold sway with the philosophers of the Enlightenment (17th and 18th centuries), and few rose to challenge it as a moral principle. Virtually none have realized that the end of altruism (hatred, looting of the individual and re-distribution of income) has always been genocidal murder of prosperous and intelligent people.

Altruism is the underlying premise for the subordination of the individual to social control. As a philosophical premise, it requires that man be controlled, presumably, so he does not fill the world with decadence and misery. This view is from the Dark Ages and should have been thrown out during the Enlightenment when men discovered that they should be free.

By nature, man's survival requires action. But it also requires a competent mind. In order to live, man acts with, and among the materials in existence. In this sense, man is unique among animals, in that he adapts reality for his own purpose, rather than adapt to it. This implies that there are materials in nature susceptible to alteration by man for purpose of survival. Indeed, it is the mind that has the ability to spur action and invent new survival tools, (for instance, energy sources) and exploit nature to invent even newer machines to benefit life. A universe of absolutes, operating according to their own natures makes up an ordered environment that can be understood and manipulated by a properly functioning consciousness. Altruism has nothing to do with survival, but egoism does.

Later, it took Ayn Rand to tell us "…man knows that his desperate need of self-esteem is a matter of life or death. As a being of volitional consciousness, he knows that he must know his own value in order to maintain his own life. He knows that he has to be right. To be wrong in action means danger to his life. To be wrong in person, to be evil, means to be unfit for existence."[17]

Since some men *choose* to think, and others choose *not* to think; it should be the role of government to protect the exercise of the rational faculty. In fact, this is the fundamental premise of a free and proper society: that man be liberated from the shackles of altruistic sacrifice.

This is done through the recognition that nature does not provide man's sustenance automatically, but such sustenance must be achieved intellectually through careful thought and action. Those products that an individual creates necessarily become his property. By protecting property rights, governments protect the right of man to make values that improve his life, and make a happy and successful life possible. Today's altruistically inclined leaders seem to have forgotten that man has a mind and that it should be left alone to prosper under its own likes.

Property rights do not derive from the premise that all men are different and would do differently

---

[17] Atlas Shrugged by Ayn Rand, This is John Galt speaking. https://amzn.to/3mFjo9R (Paid link)

with similar types of property. That is the conservative argument. In truth, property rights derive from man's productive nature; and since production is an ethical, moral requirement of life, property rights should be the most fundamental ethical principle in political theory.

During the Enlightenment, and on into modern times, the ultimate enemy for altruists was property rights and capitalism. As social institutions, both concepts represent freedom and the pursuit of happiness as opposed to monarchical rule and the King's prerogative.[18] Monarchies and dictatorships routinely suppress capitalism and free trade because such suppression provides them with the scapegoat they need to advance to centralized government. This scapegoat is the productive individual who must be destroyed in order to advance theft of property and denial of individual rights.

Altruism holds that anything done for personal gain is evil. That is why altruists say that virtue consists of self-sacrificial dedication. Altruism's denial of the value of capitalism means disapproval of the virtues that capitalism requires (reason, egoism, self-interest, property, and profits). Altruism brought to men a blind spot of

---

[18] "The King's prerogative refers to the ability of a monarch to delegate special rights and privileges to his favorites while also suppressing his enemies.

sorts; one that leads them to conclude there is no other way of looking at society and life except through the altruists' sacrificial visors. This releases the monsters of human sacrifice to continue their con game of ruling men through guilt, and it causes the failure of society as an institution that should regularize volitionary trade and the creation of wealth.

Altruism's view of man as a being of misery and decadence justifies its view of society as a collective institution. If man is a savage, then they feel it is proper to make him do what is right (despite himself). In order to avoid the question of "Who am I?", the altruist asks of others, "Who do you think you are?" The implication of this question goes further, however, to mean, "Who do you think you are to live, to think, to be happy, to believe you are so good as to be self-sufficient?" By this method, the altruist creates an inversion, a way of looking at virtue that draws basically innocent men down, lowering their postures, stifling their vision, and if they accept the inversion fully, turns them into animals of prey.

But man *is* a being of volition. He is not guilty or impotent by nature. In fact, volition is the singular most essential aspect of man. It is the feature that represents the basic difference between man and animals as we discussed above. Volition relates to one choice: to think or not to think[19]. The choice an individual makes on this issue determines, more than any other issue, the direction his life will take.

It takes a complete and consistent philosophy to help a man advance from the first step of human thought, which is that decision to think. It takes an understanding of reason and of the way it operates for a man's consciousness to take the second step (which is to use reason). It takes a further advance to the discovery of the virtues that proceed from a recognition of man's nature (specifically from the facts of man's type of consciousness as it relates to reality). Finally, it takes a singular purpose, a goal, in order for a man to practice those virtues and accomplish his purpose. The next step is production.

It is important to understand the devastating consequences of the altruist morality on human thriving. If a man chooses to be moral, but is given the injunctions of a code of ethics (altruism) not consistent with his nature as man--for instance, if he holds charity as more important than productiveness--his efforts to live a life of virtue will produce the opposite of his self-interest.

---

[19] A principle developed by Ayn Rand

This difference (between altruism and virtuous living) shows that productiveness is by far the better virtue compared to sacrifice. Creating innovative products actually accomplishes (for man and society) the values that were supposed to have come from altruism's never-arriving utopia. The virtue of production, if allowed to flourish, will improve society in a way far more effective than the "virtue" of giving up your values. Production is the virtue that *improves* society. Altruism destroys the virtue of productiveness while it destroys society.

The desire for the good in morality is sabotaged by the injunction that man should sacrifice for others. In fact, the rejection of altruism, when it happens, will lift a veil over human knowledge and release man to live productively and, most importantly, will give him the knowledge he needs to fight against the theft of his product. To live without guilt is to live without altruism.

On the other hand, if altruism continues the destruction of the good, it will pit man against his own nature, thereby destroying the possibility of his achieving true virtue. In fact, it is a common tactic of many cultural elites to admonish the basically good man for his "bad" streak of individuality. The goal of such admonitions is to prevent the good man from discovering the nature of the ego. Such people do not want man to realize his nature as a being of self-sufficient ego, so they advocate schemes and moral codes that exhort man to deny his own nature for the sake of someone else's opinion of what is moral.

It is within this context that we learn that altruism does not mean benevolence and good will among men. Altruism is the philosophy that tells a man that his prime motive and highest virtue is to live for other men. Its purpose is to engender guilt in basically good men and turn them into willing slaves. One telling feature of altruism is that it does not hold productive virtues as primary and that they proceed from the choice to think.

To the extent that altruism gives lip service to productive virtues, it is for the purpose of keeping the victim alive for as long as possible. But as is the goal of any thief or murderer, the goal of altruistic incantations is this: to destroy any vestige of the good, to obliterate from this earth the image of a man of independent judgment, to kill the independence in man. It is precisely such motivation that causes the predominance of the view that man's sole purpose is to live for the tribe or society.

If man does survive by means of reason, then he must be protected against those who would survive by unreason. This is why man is held to have certain inalienable rights, rights that inhere in man's nature that cannot be violated by any man. The protection of property rights is the implementation of the right to life, and it is property rights that, above all, provide the political expression of the idea of liberty.

The repudiation of altruism is the culmination of our struggle for freedom and the promise of the Declaration of Independence. This repudiation opens the door, or should I say, makes room for, egoism which is implied in our founding documents. It elevates the power of ideas and the ability of the mind to effect good living for individuals.

ESG as an Altruist Scam

I recently watched a commercial offering a service to help companies get into better compliance with ESG. I was disgusted that any company would think submitting to fascism was a good thing. Indeed, the implication of fascism within an ESG framework is palpable and I am not ashamed to oppose such a destructive notion. Generally, ESG is called a "management and analysis framework to understand and measure how sustainably an organization is operating."[20] ESG is an acronym that stands for Environmental, Social, and Governance. The acronym is designed to provide corporate measurements integrated around the accomplishment of environmental goals, socialist principles and a fascist alliance between government and corporations.

As such, ESG is a scam whose goal is to insinuate socialism into our economic frameworks and bring about programs that divert corporations from their proper goals of advancing "shareholder" interests and profits while replacing them with the goal of advancing "stakeholder" interests. This is a way of subversively destroying capitalism and replacing it with corporatism which is another term for fascism.

The proponents of ESG ignore the fact that ESG is a virulent form of corporate acquiescence to

---

[20] https://corporatefinanceinstitute.com/resources/esg/esg-environmental-social-governance/

governmental management. I call it corporate capture and destruction of capitalism. The proponents of ESG use flowery verbiage to portray ESG as a benevolent idea that will bring human sacrifice which is a feature of altruism. What they ignore is the fact that altruism has never yielded positive benefits for society as it has been practiced by socialism, communism, and fascism throughout history.

ESG is nothing more than another example of trying to re-brand coercive society into something that it never was intended to be. Communism is merely one of many examples of an altruist society that has been re-branded repeatedly only to arrive, again, as pragmatism, to a society that kills millions of people in order to cleanse society of self-interest and egoism (capitalism).

ESG is a sinister attempt to destroy capitalism by destroying corporations (and their proper purpose of serving the interests of shareholders). ESG seeks to divert profits (from their proper use as investments) toward a distorted form of "cooperation" that leads to governmental control of society.

To understand this, we must recognize how capitalism works in society. Capitalism is an economic system that runs efficiently when it is not interfered with by any authority, including the authority of government. Capitalism inaugurates into society the principle of property rights and the liberation of the pursuit of happiness. Capitalism requires freedom and reason and free markets.

This may be hard for technocrats to understand because they don't know that capitalism is freedom (and that individuals are always better at deciding what is in their interest). Fascism releases such technocrats into the workings of corporations (who pretend to have a faux wisdom about what companies must do to accomplish the collectivist goals of government). These unelected "technocrats" are essentially "little dictators" who disregard the rights of individuals, CEOs, and managers, forcing them against their wills.

Yet, these technocrats don't understand how to run economies or even companies. Most of them have no corporate experience and they don't know how economic principles work. The laws of economics and free markets are corrupted by the imposition of ESG that insinuates technocracy and economic failure.

The clearest statement of the flaws of ESG are found in the historical fact that governments routinely violate the law of supply and demand which is why socialist planners have routinely failed at running society. The calculations of supply and demand are best accomplished by the individual business person looking at his own business (as opposed to government agencies that regulate and control supply and demand). Such government calculations are always wrong, and society winds up with too many of some products and too few of other products.

Governments also destroy the free flow of capital to proper uses, which destroys companies. ESG technocrats also demand that companies make decisions based upon the interests of people who are not interested in the bottom lines of the companies. They get away with destroying the companies by invoking altruistic sacrifice and declare that it is *they*, the technocrats, who are working for the people against the companies that are working for mere profit and power. As companies start to disappear and workers lose their jobs, they declare that the goal of ESG was noble, and the companies failed because they sabotaged the principles of ESG. The truth is that ESG is nothing more than an effort to destroy profits and drain capital resources.

ESG also operates under the fallacy called "zero-sum" economics. With the zero-sum idea, it is thought that every trade has a winner and a loser, and, therefore, regulation is needed to control trades that will tip the scales in favor of one or the other trader. Because it is not true that zero-sum trades exist (across the full spectrum of a large economic system) to any great degree, trying to tip the scales, for one or the other party, actually creates winners and losers and destroys the reason for mutual trade to mutual benefit.

The opposite of capitalism is what I call the coercive society which includes socialism, communism, fascism, and theocracy. These are all based upon the altruism scam implied by the violation of supply and demand and the imposition of zero-sum economics. We will look at the three elements of ESG:

Environmental

One of our country's largest investors in ESG is a financial investment firm named BlackRock. If companies want investment from BlackRock, they must be active in reducing CO2 emissions and they must support environmental causes. Yet, environmentalism is a scam. It does not represent an advance for man and any corporation that ties its success to anything other than profits will lose in the marketplace. By advocating the establishment of inefficient (government subsidized) environmental products, ideas and services, corporations will suffer in the marketplace.[21]

---

[21] Quote: "…the mainstream knowledge system we rely on to help us evaluate what to do about the crucial issue of fossil fuels—the system that is telling us that the "experts" say we must rapidly eliminate fossil fuel use—cannot be trusted because it is operating on the anti-human, anti-energy, anti-impact framework.

"To know what to do about the crucial issue of fossil fuels, we need a full-context evaluation of continuing fossil fuel use—its full benefits and side-

The implication of the "E" in ESG is that corporations should divert profits through environmentally unsound policies that will not improve the environment. In other words, corporations that throw money at so-called "environmental solutions" are harming themselves by wasting profits; they are harming the consumer who must pay higher prices and taxes; and this causes decreased sales and harm to investors who are forced to invest in less profitable (ESG) companies.

Generally, in a free market, consumers and investors tend to avoid companies that are wasting their profits on unsound investments. Despite the fact that BlackRock is a huge investment firm, in the long run, E-style policies will ruin the company. Policies that destroy profits create a slippery slope toward more losses and poorer-quality products. The implication of ESG is that there are profits to be made from eating up profits and eliminating fossil fuels. As more and more companies are prosecuted for "ecocide", you can be sure they will commit corporate suicide.

Social

---

effects—that synthesizes the best expert research using the human flourishing framework, including the goal of advancing human flourishing (not eliminating human impact) and the "wild potential" of Earth (not the "delicate nurturer" view)." Source "Fossil Future" by Alex Epstein https://amzn.to/461Cb0J Page 109

Social justice is a goal supposedly accomplished by introducing various anti-capitalist schemes that *also* divert profits from corporations over time. Social justice is the supposed re-distribution of wealth from rich to poor. It is another altruist scheme that fails to accomplish its end, as we have discussed. This is why BlackRock rates ESG in the companies it offers to clients. When companies divert their profits to the goal of re-distribution, of any type, the result is stolen profits and corporate decline. This policy will fail, just like every socialist scheme in history has failed.

Governance

The implication here is the corporate/government alliance, another name for fascism. What BlackRock seeks here is the appearance of cooperating with the government. For instance, if the government writes a law that companies should set up internal programs for "helping the poor", they must use labor hours to re-direct employees to charity work instead of production. It also "enlists" corporations to re-distribute their profits to pay for social and charity programs that will create losses for the bottom line. The actual goal of such government-imposed "charity" is for government to take over and manage the corporations. In this sense, BlackRock is a saboteur of the capitalist system on behalf of coercive centralized government. It is the victory of the state over the individual.

Overall, the result of ESG is a takeover of capitalist corporations, the loss of profits, and a decline of the capitalist system. Fink peppers corporate communications with flowery phrases about putting clients first, saving the planet, helping the poor, but, in truth, the company puts its anti-capitalist sentiments first, while it creates a deadly soup of altruistic claptrap that "forces" companies to follow a rating system that exploits its clients.

BlackRock's recipe for success is the destruction of capitalism and the resurrection of fascism. Metaphorically, Fink claims to be planting a garden, but, in reality, he is using altruism as fertilizer to turn the power of government to its benefit. Additionally, there is no proof that his intellectual pudding will taste good going down. You could look at it as a de facto shakedown racket that uses altruism to gain credibility. The ultimate goal is "corporate capture" and the government/business alliance.

In fact, the G in ESG makes possible the complete takeover of corporations around the country. What does the idea of government giving "orders" to corporations have to do with freedom? Consider the implications for surveillance and censorship in society.

Critical Race Theory as Altruism and Pseudo-Science

CRT (otherwise known as Critical Race Theory) represents a false history, historical revisionism in a sense. As I have written, "CRT is founded on a concept known as Marxist critical theory. In short, where the Marxists foster a class struggle between rich and poor, critical race theorists foster a class struggle between black and white (in which black is destined to rule the world). Remember Biden's comments that "poor kids are just as bright and just as talented as white kids," for an indication of the connection between critical race theory and rich versus poor.

CRT is a substitute racism intended to replace Marxist racial theory with a black-centered racial struggle. As such it is an anti-concept that attacks history and replaces it with a new form of struggle. CRT is an anti-historical and anti-intellectual movement seeking to overwhelm society through a new racist vision that sees only collective struggle as the dominant metaphysic. CRT is a new form of egalitarianism based upon a revised form of racism. It seeks to replace old forms of racism with a virulent hatred of all skin colors except black. CRT is skin color racism. As I have written:

"CRT is the racialization of the Marxist class struggle in the same way that critical theory was the collectivization of the class struggle. We must remember that the class struggle is an economic joining of all people (who are not wealthy) into a unity (collective) that Marxists wanted to enlist in their struggle to destroy capitalism. Likewise, critical race theory seeks to convince people that race is everywhere and enlist them in the struggle, not to destroy racism, but to destroy capitalism. Indeed, race is a social construct, but it was constructed by our modern philosophers, Marxists, and critical race theorists as an extension of their anti-capitalism.

"The fundamental premises of critical race theory are:

- Collectivism,
- Racism,
- Socialism,
- Critical Theory (class struggle),
- Pseudo-science and anti-intellectualism,
- Revisionist history based upon the "history" of skin color,
- Revolutionary Violence,
- Altruism,
- Blind Activism formulated out of Nihilism, and
- Hatred of the intelligent for being intelligent. (Edited list)

"Critical race theory is a social construct invented out of the residue of Marxist critical theory and class struggle. CRT is, in effect, the next phase of Marxist critical theory through a concept called intersectionality. CRT advocates also construct race in society by declaring a universal struggle against their invented form of racism. In reality, there is so little racism in society compared to the gargantuan that CRT makes it out to be.

"Today, race is talked about as if it is the only social division in society, the struggle between black and white (two colors that do not exist universally even among groups). When no person has "a single, easily stated unitary identity," critical race theorists will create those identities for them and make them think they are part of an iconoclastic movement that must fight against an equally invented enemy (racism). These identity groups were constructed in the universities, given "safe spaces" to vent their invented anger, maliciously manipulated to do violence against fictional enemies, and turned into warring camps that create burned out cities in the name of "peaceful protests."

"As we suggest, critical theory is a method for insinuating the Marxist critique of capitalism into the educational system through pseudo-scientific sociological (and peer-reviewed) studies that insinuate collectivism and sacrifice of the individual to society.

"Make no mistake about it; these new walls between the "races" are not about solving race issues. There will never come a time when racism goes away under critical race theory. In fact, CRT is a mechanism intended to keep race in the forefront of political debate. What they intend is to intellectually enslave the mind of men by indoctrinating the children into becoming racist haters. Their goal is not freedom but the elevation of racism in society.

"Intersectionality represents "the complex, cumulative way in which the effects of multiple forms of discrimination (such as racism, sexism, and classism) combine, overlap, or intersect especially in the experiences of marginalized individuals or groups. (My comment: What this means is that skin color discrimination is made into a fundamental metaphysical principle, a wider principle of reality than racism, sexism and classism.)

""[Kimberlé] Crenshaw introduced the theory of intersectionality, the idea that when it comes to thinking about how inequalities persist, categories like gender, race, and class are best understood as overlapping and mutually constitutive rather than isolated and distinct. — Adia Harvey Wingfield"[22]

"The idea of intersectionality between various political groups is intended to "collect" (or hide) such groups into a singular struggle not against

---

[22] https://www.merriam-webster.com/dictionary/intersectionality

racism, genderism, or classism but against capitalism.

"Note that whenever people use race, gender, or class as clubs, they utilize the same overgeneralized groupings that were born out of modern philosophy (as we have shown). These groupings are based upon the concept of collectivism as if it were unquestionable and ubiquitous. Media and culture glorify emotionalism and hatred and portray capitalist society as vicious, racist, and unjust. Hence, the Marcusean view that capitalists are bigots who enjoy capitalist production.

"Then, after making various false arguments about how collectivism intersects in society, they offer and imply that altruism, the sacrifice of the individual for the collective, is the only moral solution. They excoriate society and individuals for not choosing to sacrifice for intersectionality and collectivism and they demand the insinuation of altruistic self-sacrifice as the key principle of society.

"When you assume that everything is collectivist in nature, you will only see collectivism, and this provides the basis for critical race theory that only sees racism. If you habitually analyze society using a collective foundation, all of your "observations" will be collective – the individual does not exist, and children especially must be overwhelmed and forced to join the collective with anger, emotion, and revenge in their hearts. Everything becomes race, gender, and sexual preference to the explicit exclusion of independent minds.

"All, or any, interpretations based upon the individual and his sovereignty, his individual rights, are swept away by CRT as meaningless. He or she is portrayed as oblivious compared to the value of the collective, and, most importantly, his society (capitalism) must be portrayed as endemically racist and evil.

"The first thing you hear street activists say, when they justify their riots, fires, destructions, and murders, is that they are fighting against "systemic" racism. These criminals justify their violence using solely collectivist and altruist thinking. They are not burning and killing because they want to liberate individuals or stop discrimination. They talk only of the pragmatism of altruism; everything is about their feelings, their need to overcome society so they can steal the trappings of property and capital for themselves. Their perceptions are necessarily true, they think, because they perceive society to be evil.

"Note the next buzzword. A "marginalized" group is the next invented collective. How are people marginalized? They are supposedly blocked from success by, you guessed it, racism. This buzzword is thrown around indiscriminately in the media, the universities and even the grade schools without proof, without study, without science. A group is marginalized by social status and skin color – that's it.

"The idea of a marginalized group is contradicted by the many individuals with dark skin who succeed in society. Many of these individuals reject critical race theory and prefer to live as free individuals. They see the advocates of CRT as blocking their success by insisting that they join the "race" and engage in destruction. …

"This proves that critical race theorists have created these buzzwords of intersectionality, racism, marginalization, etc. in order to exploit individualism and use collectivism as a cudgel for the acquisition of power. The goal of CRT is, as I have written, not to solve racism, but to gain power. At base, CRT is a political tool for the progressive elites who seek political ascent. If they can convince people they are doing a "good" thing in their fight against racism, then they can insinuate their collectivist solutions into society, higher taxes, government spending, money laundering, crime, murder, and theft. CRT is a get rich quick scheme, not a serious movement. It uses the trappings of collectivism and altruism to pretend to be doing good.

"The educational upshot is that both critical theory and critical race theory trap the mind of the vulnerable student into an anti-capitalist critique ... CRT is not about race - it is about indoctrination of certain "classes" and "races" into hatred and disruption of capitalism.

"Ryan Very tells us in a footnote to his article quoted above:

""Critical race theorists investigate the underpinnings of race and racism. Many of them believe that majoritarian presuppositions, received wisdoms, and shared cultural understandings of race reinforce the status-quo conception of race and are a princip(al) obstacle to racial reform. Four basic tenets of critical race theory are that racism is ordinary, that race is socially constructed, that minorities are racialized according (to) shifting needs such as the labor market, and anti-essentialism, the view that no person has a single, easily stated unitary identity. See Delgado and Stefancic 1997: 462-463, 2001: 3-4."[23]

"To advance CRT, you need only make up arguments against capitalism, tell these newly defined identities that they are the victims of capitalism as a group, that their enemy is any light skinned individual and you can justify any criminal act as a defense against any form of "racism" that does not exist. CRT is a shell

---

[23] Hume's Essay "Of National Character" Source: https://www.econlib.org/library/LFBooks/Hume/hmMPL.html?chapter num=26#aa10

game. It is a fantasy made up by people who have no connection to reality, who feel guilty for their own wealth, and who pretend to be protecting the "marginalized." Marginalized by whom? By them.

"The meaning of "race" can also be manipulated in the struggle against capitalism. Marginalized groups intersect on the streets. Today it is women who are marginalized, tomorrow blacks, gays, trans people, Native Americans, etc. The protesters are all the same people – that is the essence of intersectionality – collectivization of invented groups.

"Notice that most of the protestors and rioters are not poor. They make their money by protesting on behalf of mega billionaires – agitation is their profession (thanks to Obama and his ilk). The real beneficiaries are the multi-billionaires who are footing the bill and putting themselves out of business for the sake of what? A better society?

"This explains why you are seeing riots and destructions in the American street today. These rioters are the equivalent of the Nazi brownshirts who destroyed shops and businesses in pre-war Germany. Today's anti-capitalist disruptions of society, utilizing racial innovations, set the terms for the communist takeover of America that Marcuse and his children advocated.

"In asserting these racial divisions (rich kids who masquerade as "the poor" victims of capitalism),

CRT also creates a decline in educational standards because it traps students, teachers, and textbooks into a new Marxist (false) critique and "forces" students to decline intellectually when they see everything through skin color. Where fascist racial theory turned Germany's educational system into the worship of the pseudo-science of race theory, today's critical race theorists, turn education into the pseudo-science of skin color."[24]

---

[24] "The Scourge of Racism and the Cure by Robert Villegas https://amzn.to/3kLBVQQ (Paid link)

Altruism as a Money Laundering Device

The term used for altruism as a money laundering device is called effective altruism. As a proponent of effective altruism, SBF (Sam Bankman Fried) declared that he was using his profits to advance altruistic social schemes. This, according to him, would make society a better place as altruistic goals made society better. This was a lie.

The idea of justifying your promises for a better society through massive amounts of altruistic giving cannot be "validated" if we evaluate the results objectively. The idea of altruism and the promise to help people through the use of other peoples' money is a philosophical and moral dead end.

Those who advocate being motivated by altruism (helping people) are trying to convince people that their motivations are noble and that their altruistic actions are morally validated. This is the case with SBF and any other charlatan who wants to take other peoples' money under the guise of helping people. These charlatans are among a group of people who use altruism as a way of "making" money to enrich themselves.

We have in society a group of like-minded people working to bring about their own enrichment. This disparate group is an actual conspiracy because they use the same ideologies to advance similar goals. They need only use the same arguments to cover their altruistic giving. These arguments come from the Bible, Immanuel Kant, and the sundry college professors who have written books about effective altruism (Note, they all advocate socialism; they all advocate central government, they all advocate high taxes taken from individuals for the sake of paying for government programs).

For instance, in a mixed economy[25] (or a socialist system), the advocates of the system seldom meet to advance socialism, yet, their combined acts, generally, accomplish this result. These individuals are joined, at first, in college and are educated by professors (generally) who follow the ideas of Kant, Hume, Hegel, Dewey, and Pierce. These philosophers generally work to gaslight the minds of men about the value of "giving", while also advocating altruism (giving to the poor as in Marxism), and they invent various means to denigrate capitalism and individual liberties. Within the milieu of this group of socialists are specific individuals who rise to the top of the "totem pole", so to speak. These individuals are involved in virtually every sphere of influence and rise to the top with the help of fellow travelers in other fields. These individuals see the rising tide of socialism (within the framework of modern

---

[25] A "mixed economy" is an economy that operates on the basis both of coercive measures (such as regulations, taxation, social justice) and economic freedom. Such a society swings back and forth as separate elements in society strive politically to mitigate the consequences of force and freedom.

philosophy), and receive accolades for their political skills. These individuals, the power brokers and the artists who are given the red carpet, are disseminators of anti-capitalism and indoctrination.

The common strategy of the left involves the creation of pseudo-emergencies intended to stress the social system until it breaks. This sets the stage for their offering socialism as the solution. Pseudo-emergencies such as "climate change", the "failures of capitalism", and self-interest are created by these people and used to manipulate the citizenry and destroy their lives.

For instance,
- Larry Fink and BlackRock
- George Soros and Open Society Foundation
- Klaus Schwab and the WEF
- Josh Bolton and the Business Roundtable
- Sam Bankman Fried and FTX

Name: Larry Fink
Field/Company: Finance/BlackRock
Description: This company is steeped in corporate altruism. It claims to support "stakeholders" which is a general term for socialism's "downtrodden" or poor. The company uses moral force and threats of exclusion for any company that does not openly succumb to the company's ESG policies (See below).

According to a Judiciary Committee letter to BlackRock (July 6, 2023), "BlackRock is the world's largest asset manager, with over $9 trillion of assets under management as of March 31, 2023. As of the end of 2021, BlackRock owns 7.7% of the shares and casts 9.8% of the votes of the entire Standard and Poor's (S&P) 500. Together with State Street Corporation and The Vanguard Group, Inc., BlackRock is one of the so-called "Big Three" asset managers that own a combined 21.9% and vote a combined 24.9% of the shares of the S&P 500.

"BlackRock is a member of both Climate Action 100—and the Net Zero Asset Managers initiative (NZAM). Through Climate Action 100—, BlackRock appears to have reached a collusive agreement with other institutional investors to "work with the companies in which [they] invest to…deliver [] net zero [greenhouse gas (GHG)] emissions by 2050." Similarly, through NZAM, BlackRock appears to collusively have agreed with other asset managers to "[w]ork in partnership with asset owner clients on decarbonization goals, consistent with an ambition to reach net zero emissions by 2050 or sooner across all assets under management."

"These collusive agreements to "decarboni[ze]" and reduce emissions to net zero by 2-5- would require draconian "declines in the use of coal, oil and gas": as much as 98% for coal, 94% for oil, and 86% for fossil fuels overall. This, in turn, would require radical steps such as halting sales of new internal combustion engine passenger cars by 2035, and phasing out all unabated coal and oil power plants by 2040." It also would mean "that no new oil and gas fields must be developed," choking off investment in these industries. Such restrictions limit output and increase prices and deprive businesses of investments and consumers of choices. The potential consequences for American freedom and economic well-being are far-reaching."

On the corporate website, "Larry Fink discusses rising rates, banking sector stresses, and a fragmenting global economy – but emphasizes client choice and the importance of hope for investors." This (like Soros and others) represents altruist claptrap intended to portray the company as a social justice champion. Remember, we have argued that altruism does not work because it requires the self-sacrifice of the productive sectors of the economy for the sake of the nonproductive sectors.

BlackRock has come up with a social justice management tool in its ESG strategy. The investment firm issues ESG ratings for any business it invests in. For BlackRock, ESG is an empty investment strategy. By focusing investments on companies that subscribe to the ESG strategy, BlackRock thinks they can focus dollars on Environmental, Social, and Governance matters. You could call ESG strategy a way of identifying the companies ripe for exploitation. If you are successful and you have a good ESG rating, you are in.

BlackRock's stress on the government/business alliance also resurrects leftist politics, pragmatism, and indeterminacy into a system that skims money from corporations. In effect, they are stealing the trappings of capitalism as a way of undermining capitalism for the sake of "the planet". Again, remember that altruism doesn't work.

Let me state clearly that ESG is a destructive philosophy that cannot and does not have the clients and shareholders in mind. To put re-distributionist concepts at the forefront of corporations will destroy the company bottom lines.

The reason companies such as BlackRock exert so much pressure on corporations to adopt ESG is the philosophy of altruism. Today, both liberals and conservatives advocate altruism, the sacrifice of the individual to society. Not only are most CEOs thoroughly pragmatic when they seek to avoid being shamed by ESG, they are blind to the fact that if they challenge ESG, they will not only lose profits but also become morally corrupt.

Yet, even individuals within these corporations see altruism as a positive benefit for society. They think it is great that their companies are spending huge dollars helping the poor, completely oblivious to the fact that it is the profits they have worked to create that are paying for environmental programs that cost the economy millions of dollars annually.

Moral fear moves them to applaud ESG as it helps the government establish central planning and dictatorship. This is the mistake that is causing the decline and destruction of capitalism. Until society returns to individualism, the rights of individuals to the pursuit of happiness, the stormtroopers of altruism, Fink, and his minions, will eventually destroy society. We must challenge altruism for the evil moral system that it is. It not only destroys productive citizens, it also violates the principle that production comes before consumption. It is altruism that leads to genocide and mass murder as history has shown. How do they get away with this? Using the flowery language of love for mankind, of kindness and the beauty of giving, they slide by, pretending to be loving people who care about others, they fool productive people into giving their values to people who do not care about creating their own values. In fact, they don't realize that it is capitalism, fossil-fuel based machines, and the profit-motive that are beautifying the planet. In particular, it is fossil fuels and the machines they power that are creating abundance and human flourishing on our planet.

ESG is a fascist device used by companies that don't want to compete fairly. Their goal is to destroy capitalism under the false notion that diverting profits to charity actually does good for those corporations. Yet, the strategy that lies beneath ESG is the notion that companies that don't subscribe to the false premises of ESG should be put out of business by the government. It is a good business strategy, thinks Larry Fink, to show people that corporations are not selfish. They are instead eager to show that they hate money unless it is given away. Wait for the law of diminishing returns[26] as increases in altruistic spending grow beyond the bottom line.

BlackRock's goal is to destroy capitalism and turn society into a re-distribution industry. Anytime you force companies to divert profits to so-called stakeholders rather than shareholders, you will cause shareholders to exit, and, in the long run, BlackRock will destroy itself as each of the companies in which it invests begin to lose profits. Fink's gambit of ESG will eventually fail. It is fooling no one.

---

[26] The law of diminishing returns says that, if you keep increasing one factor in the production of goods (such as your workforce) while keeping all other factors the same, you'll reach a point beyond which additional increases will result in a progressive decline in output. In other words, there's a point when adding more inputs will begin to hamper the production process. Source: https://www.britannica.com/money/diminishing-returns

Name: George Soros
Field/Company: Finance/Open Society Foundation
Description: Soros was supposedly mentored by pragmatist philosopher Karl Popper who defined the concept of Open Society "in which individuals are confronted with personal decisions" as opposed to a "magical or tribal or collectivist society."[27]

"Among the educated general public, Popper is best known for his critique of totalitarianism and his defense of freedom, individualism, democracy and an "open society." His political thought resides squarely within the camp of Enlightenment rationalism and humanism. He was a dogged opponent of totalitarianism, nationalism, fascism, romanticism, collectivism, and other kinds of (in Popper's view) reactionary and irrational ideas."[28]

"According to Popper, totalitarianism was not unique to the 20th century. Rather, it "belongs to a tradition which is just as old or just as young as our civilization itself" (Open Society, Vol. I, 1). In The Open Society, Popper's search for the roots of totalitarianism took him back to ancient Greece. There he detected the emergence of what

---

[27] https://en.wikipedia.org/wiki/Open_society#:~:text=Karl%20Popper%20defined%20the%20open%20society%20as%20one,the%20need%20for%20bloodshed%2C%20revolution%20or%20coup%20d%27%C3%A9tat.

[28] https://iep.utm.edu/popp-pol/

he called the first "open society" in democratic Athens of the 5th century B.C.E., Athenians, he argued, were the first to subject their own values, beliefs, institutions and traditions to critical scrutiny and Socrates and the city's democratic politics exemplified this new attitude. But reactionary forces were unnerved by the instability and rapid social change that an open society had unleashed. (Socrates was indicted on charges of corrupting the youth and introducing new gods.) They sought to turn back the clock and return Athens to a society marked by rigid class hierarchy, conformity to the customs of the tribe, and uncritical deference to authority and tradition—a "closed society."

"This move back to tribalism was motivated by a widely and deeply felt uneasiness that Popper called the "strain of civilization." The structured and organic character of closed societies helps to satisfy a deep human need for regularity and a shared common life, Popper said. In contrast, the individualism, freedom, and personal responsibility that open societies necessarily engender leave many feeling isolated and anxious, but this anxiety, Popper said, must be born(e) if we are to enjoy the greater benefits of living in an open society: freedom, social progress, growing knowledge, and enhanced cooperation. "It is the price we have to pay for being human" (Open Society Vol. 1, 176)."[29]

Popper's philosophy merely gave Soros cover to associate open society with modern forms of "democracy" which included a socialism for which we can vote. For instance, it is said of Popper: ("So, what did Popper mean by 'the open society'? A good way to answer the question is with reference to his work in the philosophy of science, for which he is just as well-known as he is for his work in political philosophy. Popper's contribution to the philosophy of science is his doctrine of 'falsificationism', according to which science proceeds by formulating hypotheses and attempting to falsify them by experimental tests (which is clearly based upon Hume's concept of necessity). On this view, it is impossible to demonstrate, with certainty, that any given hypothesis is true; that is, to 'verify' it conclusively. The best you can ever do is rule it out as false. (Last parenthesis mine)

"(Falsificationism is Popper's response to the 'verificationism' espoused by the Vienna Circle, which met in Popper's home city in the years before World War Two.) It is a view which portrays the scientist as having to exercise certain virtues: creativity and imagination in the formulation of theories and hypotheses, as well as

---

[29] https://iep.utm.edu/popp-pol/#H2

in devising experiments with which to test them; critical rationality in the assessment of theories and other claims; the toleration required to recognise that other peoples' theories could be rivals to your own. (Popper is popular with many scientists I know. No wonder when he makes science sound so exciting.)

"An 'open society', then, is a society characterised by institutions which make it possible to exercise the same virtues in the pragmatic pursuit of solutions to social and political problems. For Popper, these are, pretty much, the institutions characteristic of a modern liberal democracy."[30] (Notice the term "pragmatic". Popper fit in very well with American pragmatists. One could say, he fathered their ideas as they flowered from Hume's view of necessity, and Kant's indeterminism.)

Soros was so influenced by Popper that he adopted the open society concept as his own and tried to bring it about through an investment philosophy bent on "reflexivity", the herd movement of mindless investors who think that following Soros is the equivalent to productive investment – which brings forward the ability of Soros to sell short to their detriment.

---

[30] https://philosophynow.org/issues/38/The_Open_Society_Revisited#:~:text=An%20%E2%80%98open%20society%E2%80%99%2C%20then%2C%20is%20a%20society%20characterised,the%20institutions%20characteristic%20of%20a%20modern%20liberal%20democracy.

But the concept of an open society is not the equivalent of a free society in the sense that we know it today. In the Soros scheme, an open society is more closely linked to a pure democracy in which society decides all actions by means of the citizens' votes; but this too is not exactly correct. Soros' Open Society is a socialist dictatorship brought about by Soros money and grants from the U.S. government. For instance, the Open Society Foundation worked in Ukraine to fund protests against the government, change the government and also work with the U.S. State Department to prosecute companies competing in the Ukrainian energy industry (against Soros). Open Society is a socialist experiment based upon the Soros investment strategy. In effect, Soros claimed to be working for a better society. In fact, whenever Soros was questioned about his "meddling" in other countries, he claimed to be doing selfless altruism and accused critics of being antisemitic. I have observed that very few so-called "conspiracy theorists" have opposed Soros because he was Jewish. It is more about his meddling in the electoral process (in America) that he admits he is doing.

In the USA, Soros is the biggest campaign financier of Democratic Party politicians. He has also funded the campaigns of various leftist prosecutors who have worked to release thousands of violent criminals that has disrupted the American justice system. So much for making a better society.

Soros' Open Society is very much like Fink's ESG. For an investor to be engaged in a strategy of creating a socialist system cannot be called anything but corrupt. In the Soros Open Society, scientists would be allowed to do the "science thing" but they could never do anything more than take "bold leaps" into action, and, like most "pragmatic" action, these bold leaps could only be evaluated after the results had come in. Only the elite among investors, men such as Soros, could drive average investors toward "bubbles" and ascertain when to sell short. At that point Soros would have "everything manipulated".[31]. Never believe a Soros economic prediction without reading between the lines. My suggestion is to run as fast as you can.

The fact that Soros has been a predatory manipulator of politicians, journalists and Presidents was offered to society as a boon – when, in truth, Soros had always been working, not for the betterment of society, but for the financial betterment of his clients. By encouraging these people to work for Soros' own "business/government alliance", Soros is, like Fink, working to establish fascism. He thought he

---

[31] A common conspiracy theory about Soros' purported intentions.

might be a god because of his own stochastic narcissism.

Name: Klaus Schwab

Field/Organization Name: Global Technology/World Economic Forum (WEF)

Description: WEF is a major organization of powerful and rich individuals who want to create a business/government alliance (fascist state). Its goal is to control the lives of individuals using advanced technological means that would organize society into a new industrial revolution. The historical equivalents of the WEF are the early Marx-inspired communist organizations that believed you could take over the factories built by the capitalists and use them to create the perfect socialist man. They believed that the factories built by capitalists would be just as productive once taken over by people who preferred to skim profits they did not know how to make.

"Klaus Schwab, the founder of the World Economic Forum, which famously meets every year in Davos, Switzerland, is advising a "Great Reset" of economic policy as a way of recovering from the effects of the COVID-19 pandemic and addressing climate change. This will require that we "reconsider our collective commitment to 'capitalism' as we have known it", and acknowledge that consumers are allegedly more interested in corporate-sponsored social-welfare programs than in buying goods and services at a reasonable price."[32]

"The World Economic Forum is the International Organization for Public-Private Cooperation.

"The Forum engages the foremost political, business, cultural and other leaders of society to shape global, regional and industry agendas.

"It was established in 1971 as a not-for-profit foundation and is headquartered in Geneva, Switzerland. It is independent, impartial, and not tied to any special interests. The Forum strives in all its efforts to demonstrate entrepreneurship in the global public interest while upholding the highest standards of governance. Moral and intellectual integrity is at the heart of everything it does.

"Our activities are shaped by a unique institutional culture founded on the stakeholder theory, which asserts that an organization is accountable to all parts of society. The institution carefully blends and balances the best of many kinds of organizations, from both the public and private sectors, international organizations, and academic institutions. (There is that word "stakeholder" again. Are you getting the drift of the altruism that permeates all these "pie in the sky" notions here?) (Last parenthesis mine)

---

[32] https://www.nationalreview.com/2020/10/davos-chiefs-call-for-higher-taxes-more-regulation-would-mean-less-prosperity/

"We believe that progress happens by bringing together people from all walks of life who have the drive and the influence to make positive change." (The word "together" must make your interest pique – think collectivism and Open Society) (Last parenthesis mine)

The statement above is obviously self-serving, intended to make the organization appear to be non-partisan and altruistic. Yet, the statement that it is an "International Organization for Public-Private Cooperation" exposes its true nature as an organization based on fascism. As I have pointed out before, "Public-Private cooperation is founded by fascism."

Note again the usage of the term "stakeholder". This is a dog whistle for the term "socialism" and indicates that the WEF is only about the destruction of capitalism. It seeks to destroy self-interest, constitutional freedoms, and individual rights. Any corporation or individual who joins the WEF has essentially pledged to advocate a Marxist future and social failure. Judging from Schwab's book "The Great Reset", this organization is basically an oligarchy seeking to enslave the individual on behalf of the elites who run the WEF. They claim a pragmatist and utilitarian perspective (so do all the other organizations involved with these groups), but they are liars and thieves and elitist snobs who hate you for being on this earth. Once they establish a digital currency, the promises will stop, and the thieving will begin. This organization is so inept that it will never accomplish anything but Sri Lanka-style poverty and starvation[33].

Name: Joshua Bolton

Field/Organization Name: Corporate Business Association/Business Roundtable

Description: If your previous concept of a corporation (as a profit-seeking organization) is under attack, should you go back to economic basics or just follow the crowd? In fact, many corporate leaders feel so guilty for seeking profits today they declare hatred for profits. For them, the problem is nagging threats from the government (antitrust, regulations, bad publicity, etc.) that view corporations as greedy and selfish.

---

[33] "An island nation of 22 million people, Sri Lanka used to be self-sufficient in food. But President Gotabaya Rajapaksa's drive to make the country the world's first to fully adopt organic agriculture – by banning all synthetic agrochemicals, including fertilisers and pesticides – has proved disastrous for Sri Lanka's food security…

"The country's 2 million farmers, who make up 30 percent of its labour force and who until then were dependent on subsidised chemical fertilisers, suddenly found themselves left to their own devices. They said the government neither increased production of organic fertiliser nor imported sufficient soil nutrients to meet their needs." Source: https://www.aljazeera.com/news/2022/5/18/a-food-crisis-looms-in-sri-lanka-as-farmers-give-up-on-planting#:~:text=An%20island%20nation%20of%2022%20million%20people%2C%20Sri,has%20proved%20disastrous%20for%20Sri%20Lanka%E2%80%99s%20food%20security.

Recently, the CEOs of the Business Roundtable have taken a bold new leap by changing the definition of the corporation (and insinuating altruism and collectivism within that definition). Remember what Dr. Peikoff said: They are merely making "a pronounced slant to the left" ...as the country moves further to the left in general, the pragmatists are carried along."

In fact, many of the ideas coming out of universities today involve a strong hatred of self-interest, capitalism, and profits. Advocates of altruism (socialists, communists, fascists, and pragmatists) excoriate CEOs for being selfish and predatory. The result is that CEOs who feel guilty for being "capitalists" often promise to give away their profits or do other things to pay homage to the social justice crowd now infiltrating the markets (as leftist consultants).

Indeed, the idea that the end (solving a problem) justifies the means (indoctrinating the shareholders) requires setting all opposition aside and forcing it to accept new altruistic trends and floating abstractions such as ESG and DEI (Diversity, Equity, and Inclusion).

Changing the definition of the corporation is a monumental move supposedly justified by economic conditions. Yet, there is only one reason for it. It is simply a public relations move. It is a pragmatist tactic designed to politically disenfranchise free market advocates and conservatives.

No opposing argument stands a chance against the steamrolling of opinion being practiced by leftists today in organizations such as the Business Roundtable. It is convenient for them that they routinely use altruism and the appeal to "doing good" in order to justify turning society into slaves and masters. The entire nation must now christen the new definition of the corporation and fall in line with the massive government-inspired giveaway of corporate profits. Everything will be just fine, they think, if we force a change in our models of thinking. Dis-information (called "truth" by the left) is the enemy of the left while social justice, anti-trust prosecutions, regulations, re-distribution, gender wars, race wars, critical race theory, riots, property destruction, and stakeholder value are the new "truths". We must jail the purveyors of dis-information in order to save the society that is crumbling into rubble around us.

If you doubt that Business Roundtable membership is made up of dupes for the politicians, consider these words: "those at the very top, the richest individuals and the richest corporations are going to pay more" (Warren), "we're going to stand up to the greed and corruption and price fixing of the pharmaceutical industries" (Sanders), "I have proposed…that we, by 2028, cut all carbon emissions from new buildings, by 2030, carbon emissions from cars, and by 2035, all carbon emissions from the manufacture of electricity" (Warren), "as long as Washington is paying more attention to money than it is to our future, we can't make the changes we need to make. We have to attack the corruption head on" (Warren).

Don't be surprised that most CEOs in this country agree with all of these statements. Don't be surprised that our government gets bigger and more oppressive every day while CEOs know that if they disagree with these statements, they are doomed (They are doomed anyway).

The pragmatists in the business world went to school with the pragmatists in government. In the real world, a corporation is made up of departments, business units and managers that work cooperatively to achieve *shareholder* value. If any action within the corporation detracts from that goal, it is seen as counterproductive and harmful to corporate value. Shareholders, seeing inefficiencies, would perceive the loss of value and take their investments elsewhere. This is called the movement of capital to better uses, a free market principle at the heart of capitalism. This hasn't changed – capitalism only works when companies focus on shareholder value – meaning profits. But the CEOs of the Business Roundtable want to change that – and to accomplish this, they must rope the shareholders into christening the new definition of the corporation as focused on "stakeholder value". Many CEOs, educated as altruists since kindergarten and all the way into Harvard and Princeton, see the corporations' need for profits as selfish and they spend lots of money to produce well-polished press releases, prospectuses, and earnings statements to convince shareholders that altruism and social responsibility are the best ways to earn profits. Like Leninists in the past, their rationalizations are intended to indoctrinate all parties that goodwill comes to the corporation through government contracts, subsidies, and government grants, not to mention beneficial legislation that improves market share. By fostering the social goals of the government, the corporation declares itself a good community partner that puts people first, not profits. How Dewey of them.

The CEOs of the Business Roundtable would likely respond to shareholder opposition by declaring they should not be expected to buck the trend toward corporate benevolence. Why should they have to take a stand against the trend of ever-growing government? One should not have to oppose a government that takes care of people, protects their environment, makes sure they have health care, childcare, free college and free everything. Why shouldn't citizens give up their guns so the government can protect them? The Business Roundtable is only doing its part in this grand scheme to create a better world. What is so bad about that? What kind of monster would oppose such benevolence?

The answer is David Hume and Immanuel Kant who "christened" the idea that knowledge of the real world was impossible.[34] What they left in their wake was Kant's morality of "duty" and the call to sacrifice (altruism) to be imposed upon us by a so-called "benevolent" government that teaches us right from wrong.

Anyone who understands that force is not the way to create a better society also knows that force, moral force, indoctrination, moralizing, and dividing people are ways to destroy society. In a capitalist system, corporate strategies work together without internal conflict. They must serve the interests of the shareholders who seek real bottom-line results. If a corporation declares that it will not seek profits alone, but also goals not directly related to profits, the shareholders will take notice. Most investors are not stupid.

---

[34] Hume declared that there is no necessity (cause and effect) because we can't see it while Kant declared that his noumenal world (the real world) was made up of things that cannot be perceived while things in the phenomenal world are unreal and consist of distortions and "filters". Both Hume and Kant shut man's mind off from reality and made it stochastic in nature – random. That is the state of the modern mind – men think randomly and disconnectedly. This "required" Dewey and the pragmatists who could only deny science and the evidence of the senses (there is no necessity) because they had no role in the life of modern man.

This is because capitalism, real capitalism, depends upon **knowledge** (to make good business decisions) and **justice** (to enable the best products and services to be created); and **self-interested moral values** to spur knowledge development, product development, better lives, self-respect, reason, objective observation, science, logic, and freedom. You can't get these values by telling people their role in life is to give up everything they do for the sake of profit skimming, theft, and money laundering. Altruism is not effective. Ask SBF.

The Business Roundtable is not made up of people who seek knowledge and justice. They don't want to win customers anymore; they want to capture them by making it impossible for the competition to flourish. This isn't capitalism but more like mercantilism, captive markets, government protectionism and conquered loot; in short, fascism. Loyalty marketing can never come before product quality.

Name: Sam Bankman Fried, AKA SBF
Field/Company: Crypto Currency Trading/FTX
Description: "**At 18:00 local time (23:00 GMT) on Monday, 12 December, officers of the Bahamas Financial Crimes Investigation Unit arrested Sam Bankman-Fried at his apartment complex, in Nassau, at the request of the US government, based on a sealed indictment filed by the Southern District of New York (SDNY).**

"The man formerly nicknamed the "King Of Crypto" has seen his company collapse, stepped down as chief executive and now faces criminal investigation.

"Over the last few years, the internet has been flooded with long interviews with him, speaking over video chat from his office desk in the Bahamas."[35]

"In a BBC radio interview, he recalled being swept up in the "effective altruism" movement. Effective altruism is a community of people "trying to figure out what practical things you can do with your life to have as much positive impact as you can on the world", he said.

"So, as Mr. Bankman-Fried recalls, he decided to get into banking to make as much money as he could to give it back to good causes.

"He learned to trade stocks during a short stint at trading firm Jane Street in New York before he got bored and decided to experiment with Bitcoin.

"He noticed the variations in the value of Bitcoin across different cryptocurrency exchanges and started arbitraging - buying Bitcoin from places selling it cheaply and selling to other places where it was trading for more."[36]

In many of his interviews, SBF declared that he had been swept up in a frenzy over the idea of "effective altruism" and he had been inspired to

---

[35] https://www.bbc.com/news/technology-63612489
[36] Ibid

do so much good that he got carried away. Yet, it will be noted that his statements about effective altruism were merely excuses to justify his crimes – just as ESG is an excuse for Larry Fink to shakedown businesses, and "Open Society" is an excuse for George Soros to manipulate governments, and the new industrial revolution is an excuse for technocrats to run our lives, and the Business Roundtable is an excuse for numerous CEO "super stars" to change the fundamental goal of the corporation – all these declarations of fealty to "helping others" are scams that will eventually install fascism (the business-government alliance) in society. These people are not saints by any means. They are the instruments of death.

Let it be known that SBF donated huge funds to the government of Ukraine to help in their fight against Russia and that many of these funds were said to have been laundered back into the Democratic party in the upshot to the 2020 elections. Thanks to SBF, large numbers of Democratic candidates for House and Senate and, likely, even candidate Biden received huge funds to help pay for commercial ads against the Republicans – using stolen money.

"Sam Bankman-Fried funneled political donations through two executives at FTX, his failed cryptocurrency exchange, to achieve bipartisan influence with both Democrats and Republicans in Washington, DC, prosecutors alleged in a new indictment Thursday.

"Bankman-Fried "did not want to be known as a left-leaning partisan, or to have his name publicly attached to Republican candidates," so he instructed two executives to donate money to certain candidates and political organizations instead, prosecutors wrote in the filing.

"The money for the donations actually came from FTX and Alameda Research, a hedge fund he also controlled, prosecutors alleged. An internal Alameda spreadsheet noted over $100 million in political contributions, according to the filing. (My comment: this made SBF the second largest doner to Democrat politicians only behind George Soros)

"Bankman-Fried "perpetuated his campaign finance scheme at least in part to improve his personal standing in Washington, D.C., increase FTX's profile, and curry favor with candidates that could help pass legislation favorable to FTX or Bankman-Fried's personal agenda, including legislation concerning regulatory oversight over FTX and its industry," prosecutors wrote in the filing.

"The details of the alleged donor scheme, which allowed Bankman-Fried to exceed contribution limits to candidates he already donated to, were detailed in a superseding indictment unsealed on Thursday, in which prosecutors elaborated on the terse indictment they'd first filed against Bankman-Fried in December.

"The original charges against Bankman-Fried included eight counts, while the updated indictment carries 12 counts, adding more conspiracy charges, including conspiracy to operate an unlicensed money-transmitting business, according to the indictment. (My comment: I wonder if these "conspiracies" will be relegated to the realm of conspiracy theories)

"Federal prosecutors in Manhattan say Bankman-Fried illegally commingled funds from FTX with Alameda Research. FTX customer funds were used for donations to political candidates, and executives lied in paperwork from the Federal Election Commissions about the source of the money, prosecutors say.

"The indictment doesn't name the co-conspirators who prosecutors allege acted as "straw donors," referring to them only as "CC-1" and "CC-2."[37]

As we have seen, one thing you can count on from each of these men is their declaration that "I wanted nothing for myself." I did it for others. It is all about "social progress" – and this is the BIG LIE being advanced by leftists and rightists who think they can get away with their thefts by invoking altruism. You can bet that what we have

---

[37] https://www.businessinsider.com/sbf-political-donations-2-executives-republicans-democrats-woke-prosecutors-2023-2?IR=T&r=US&utm_medium=referral&utm_source=yahoo.com

uncovered above is happening all over the country in dark rooms and dank corners of collapsing buildings. Indeed, altruism is the falsehood that all totalitarians use when they want to hide their evil doings. Anyone who falls for this claptrap deserves the death that will drag him into giving up his values.

It should be said that not all cultural leaders who favor altruism are in favor of dictatorship. Certainly, some leaders truly believe that altruism is the benevolent philosophy it is reputed to be. They think they are doing good things when they advance socialism in the name of ESG. They think they are working with benevolent masters when they declare their allegiance to religion, collectivism and altruism. They do not realize they are being dragged into a massive fraud. This will result in the demise of American civilization if people do not wake up to the sinister evil that altruism represents.

Likewise, church leaders and educators who advocate altruism are not necessarily evil and conniving men, trying to push us into totalitarianism's genocidal death trap. But the danger is that altruism leads men to accept unvalidated moral precepts as absolutes required by God, society, certain authority figures, the Pope and Immanuel Kant.

Altruism discourages independent thought and, therefore makes men open to the leadership of evil and conniving men. In my own case, I fought against communism in my service only to find many fraudulent pro-Communists leading our society.

Those who promise utopia and re-distribution of income (altruism) often become opportunists like Kerry, Obama, (Bill) Ayers, Sanders, AOC, and many others who are influential in society. It appears that our current leaders (circa 2030s) are working toward the destruction Ayn Rand had warned about. We are beginning the descent into the abyss.

We need only read the arguments of these types-- the communists, fascists, socialists, welfare-statists, technocrats, and other social planners--for an indication of the premise they all accept fully and with conviction--that man does not have the right to property, that if he fights for his rights, he will either starve in Siberia, burn in hell, die in gas chambers, or rot in American jails. Altruism is the money laundering scheme that will destroy our society.

The ideas of these men, the altruists who are destroying society, are based upon false promises of a more benevolent and affluent society. A knowledge system has been built up using broad duty-based anti-concepts and steamrolled collectivist lies that will entrap us all. Yet, there can be problems with knowledge systems that starve the mind of true knowledge. People begin to think they are doing good; they congratulate themselves in their use of public relations to fool the public, and they give themselves awards while the brick-and-mortar facade of duty begins to crumble.

Modern Philosophy as the Purveyor of Altruism

As I have written above, Hume declared that there is no necessity (cause and effect) because we can't see it, while Kant declares that his noumenal world (the real world) was made up of things that cannot be perceived while things in the phenomenal world are not real and consist of distortions and "filters". Both Hume and Kant shut man's mind off from reality and made it stochastic in nature – random. That is the state of the modern mind – men think randomly and disconnectedly because of philosophers such as Hume and Kant.

Kant's and Hume's minds bequeathed arbitrary randomness to the vast majority of mankind. When men's minds have been disconnected from reality, they become confused and act without direction. This is the state of most men's minds today. Their "modern" views result in genocidal murder of the human mind and body – they make the human mind into that of a willing slave.

Modern philosophy puts men into a state in which is they can barely understand their own minds and choices. Their thinking is "other-worldly" because modern philosophy is other-worldly, and most men know only shame because they cannot understand Kant and Hume.

To counter the view that the mind has been disconnected from reality, Kant invented the categories that help the noumenal mind order reality. This established a "realm" that had been ordered by the collective mind using filters (categories) built into it. This required the concept of "intuition" that was the instrument for man's wading into reality without volition – the choice to think had been revoked by the categories that further cemented the mind into the Kantian miasma of disconnectedness from reality.

Among other goals, Kant wanted to establish *a priori* status to mathematics and physics, but this approach contradicted his other goal of creating similar *a priori* concepts for the mind and its relationship with existence. He required concepts that were "transcendental", and this was his problem. The term "transcendental" consigned him effectively to the area of "idealism" and mysticism.

"Kant's exposition of the transcendental ideas begins once again from the logical distinction among categorical, hypothetical, and disjunctive syllogisms. From this distinction, as we have seen, the understanding derives the concepts of substance, cause, and community, which provide the basis for rules that obtain as natural laws within our experience. Now, from the same distinction, the reason must carry things further in order derive the transcendental ideas of the complete subject, the complete series of conditions, and the complete complex of what is possible. Thus, the "completion" of metaphysical reasoning requires transcendental ideas of three sorts, but Kant argued that each leads to its characteristic irresolvable difficulty."[38]

"Kant calls the first stage the Transcendental Aesthetic. It is about what space and time must be like, and how we must handle them, if our experience is to have the spatial and temporal properties that it has. This question about the necessary conditions of experience is for Kant a 'transcendental' question and the strategy of proceeding by trying to find answers to such questions is, as we said, the strategy of transcendental argument.

"Here Kant advances one of his most notorious views: that whatever it is that impinges on us from the mind-independent world does not come located in a spatial nor even a temporal matrix (A37=B54fn.). Rather, it is the mind that organizes this 'manifold of raw intuition', as he called it, spatially and temporally. The mind has two pure forms of intuition, space, and time, built into it to allow it to do so. ('Pure' means 'not derived from experience'.)

---

[38] http://www.philosophypages.com/hy/5g.htm

"These claims are very problematic. For example, they invite the question, in virtue of what is the mind constrained to locate a bit of information at one spatial or temporal location rather than another? Kant seems to have had no answer to this question (Falkenstein 1995; Brook 1998). Most commentators have found Kant's claim that space and time are only in the mind, not at all in the mind-independent world, to be implausible.

"The activity of locating items in the 'forms of intuition', space and time, is one of the three kinds of what Kant called synthesis and discussed in the chapter on the Transcendental Deduction. It is not entirely clear how the two discussions relate."[39]

"The "phenomenal" world, said Kant, is not real: reality, as perceived by man's mind is a distortion. The distorting mechanism is man's conceptual faculty: man's basic concepts (such as time, space, existence) are not derived from experience or reality, but come from an automatic system of filters in his consciousness (labeled "categories" and "forms of perception") which impose their own design on his perception of the external world and make him incapable of perceiving it in any manner other than the one in which he does perceive it. This proves, said Kant, that man's concepts are only a delusion, but a collective delusion which no one has the power to escape.

---

[39] https://plato.stanford.edu/entries/kant-mind/#1

Thus reason and science are "limited," said Kant; they are valid only so long as they deal with this world, with a permanent, pre-determined collective delusion (and thus the criterion of reason's validity was switched from the objective to the collective), but they are impotent to deal with the fundamental, metaphysical issues of existence, which belong to the "noumenal" world. The "noumenal" world is unknowable; it is the world of "real" reality, "superior" truth and "things in themselves" or "things as they are"— which means: things as they are not perceived by man." – Ayn Rand, *For the New Intellectual*

There is no proof that reality is divided between the noumenal and phenomenal realms. How did Kant know this? Isn't his own mind limited in this way too? If men are limited in their cognition, then isn't Kant also limited in the same way that makes it impossible for him to know it. If we can know only the *a priori*, how can he know the *a posteriori*?

Since we have already discussed how Kant and Hume insinuated indeterminacy in the chapter "Kantianism, Menticide, and Altruism" above, we know that they created the stochastic mind which left man confused and unhappy.

This stochastic mind induced by modern philosophy can be compared to being drunk on alcohol or drugs. Its connections to the mystical mindset, and the Kantian mind set, essentially make man drunk, cause him to wander through life confusedly, and without purpose. Many such "drunk" people don't know who they are supposed to be, how they are supposed to act, how to assert their personalities, or even what their personalities are supposed to be.

Their thinking is based upon two premises: the anti-mind and the anti-man. There is virtually nothing else to understand about modern ideas. When you read Hume, Kant, and their sundry students, you will note that their ideas are a miasma of confused, disconnected, and brutally dishonest ideas like none other in history.

Most of the thinkers of modern philosophy are intellectual second handers. They want the world to love them, and they think their machinations will lead to their being appreciated. Yet, the reason they are unappreciated is because their ideas amount to nothing, and the results of their ideas are confusion and self-doubt among men. They don't want to kill people, but their ideas have destroyed lives. Their need to destroy the mind is based upon the false idea that this destruction will save it. Politically, they are fascists following the tenets of pragmatism. To explain this, I will quote a section from my book "Left versus Right – A False Choice"[40]:

"Pragmatism is the philosophy of the indeterminate. It should surprise no one that virtually every recent President on both sides of the aisle has declared pragmatism as the way to get things done. Indeed, many of them have been duped by pragmatism, thinking that this particular philosophy is "all-American" because it was developed by American philosophers dedicated to practical action. Nothing could be further from the truth. I have written about the fallacies of pragmatism in more than one book. For the sake of not repeating myself, I'll reprint a segment of some of the fallacious features of pragmatism here:

""Pragmatism and its sources and offshoots came to dominate the "knowledge" produced by the greatest universities. The students taught in universities like Harvard, Princeton, even Notre Dame, Oxford and Cambridge are considered to be best prepared for success in the modern world. Yet, they are taught that knowledge is a social product, that certainty is uncertain, and that truth can only be measured by its unmeasurable results in public opinion polls and focus groups. The end result of all this measuring is the final "good," the

---

[40] Left versus Right – A False Choice by Robert Villegas https://amzn.to/43Z1RtY (Paid link)

desire and motivation of "the socialized man" to sacrifice for his fellow man. That's it; that's what all these great minds are aiming at – the morality of religion.

""Why would a group that calls itself "patriotic" do the very things that would bring down its government? Why would people who claim to love freedom encourage citizens to sacrifice their morality and production in such a way that they destroy the nation they claim to love? If we are ever going to be free again, we must reject human sacrifice rather than defend it.

""Those of us who do not get educated at the finest universities envy those who do. Most often we find ourselves the victims of guilt and self-sacrifice. We spend our lives afraid of what people think of us and promise to pay more in taxes in order to deal with the "fact" that we don't deserve our incomes and surpluses. What everyone, and I mean everyone, misses is that our political and economic principles are all fallacies. We think we can spend ourselves into prosperity while we look for bailout after bailout, stimulus after stimulus completely oblivious to the fact that these policies (taught at Harvard as enlightened) are going to cause a major collapse – because they are unrealistic and unworkable."[41]

"It should be noted, again, that virtually every modern President, has boasted that his pragmatism is a solid reason to vote for him. In fact, as pragmatists, many conservative leaders have routinely sought power by using the same arguments as those used by progressives. For instance, Donald Trump, in his second run for President, has declared essentially a pragmatist philosophy by promising additional massive spending to build cities, subsidize families, remove ugly buildings, etc.
"Likewise, today's average business executive rationalizes his or her acceptance of social justice with the argument that social justice policies will help the company gain more business, despite the fact that cooperating with anti-capitalists and Marxists means the eventual descent into altruistic self-sacrifice for our country. In fact, you will find some American CEOs praising communists and other anti-capitalists by nominating them for high office, and declaring them to be morally superior to their own corporations. If you don't see that this wipes out individualism, free speech, free choice, and any dissent against dictatorship, then you need to take another look at the history of the

---

[41] Understanding the Modern Mind by Robert George https://amzn.to/3pQlC5g (Paid link)

last century that was filled with pragmatists, communists, and saboteurs.

"It was during the 1930s that American tycoons paid for and built the Soviet Union because they sympathized with their goal of human sacrifice. Many American businesspeople bought into Marxism while others had bought into the fascism of the Nazi government. Very little has changed in this regard.

"Many American tycoons supported the goals of the Nazis, and they played a role as participants in the government/business alliance, believing that fascism was superior to capitalism. Today, the business tycoons participating in the Business Roundtable are once again building the government/business alliance that is a form of fascism based upon the philosophy of pragmatism.

"Why did so many prominent Americans do this in the time before World War 2? We must understand that, at this early stage of economic knowledge, fascism was falsely seen by progressives as an idea that promised powerful economic benefits for society. The idea that government could "engineer" economic prosperity by directing businesses to act in certain ways was accepted by many college educated individuals under the name of "technocracy." Many American educators idealized the idea of political force as an effective means for improving society.

"This was before the atrocities of fascism were known and only a few intellectuals, such as Heinrich Heine were warning of the devastation to come.

"Additionally, these tycoons were not capitalists in the full sense of the term; but they were beneficiaries of what little capitalism was allowed to exist at the time. They acted more like mercantilists seeking to establish the political environment that would enable them to corner markets and eliminate competitors[42]. They were not pure mercantilists either, but they favored the use of government and military might to secure their economic power all over the world. They became enamoured of the idea that fascism was much more efficient, powerful, and successful than capitalism because it meant the cooperation of two powerful forces: capitalist manufacturing capacity and the powerful coercion of government.

"A fascist government, during the 1930s, was thought to be the best way to increase the efficiency of an economy. Looking back, we now

---

[42] Mercantilism was an economic system of trade that spanned from the 16th century to the 18th century. Mercantilism is based on the principle that the world's wealth was static, and consequently, many European nations attempted to accumulate the largest possible share of that wealth by maximizing their exports and by limiting their imports via tariffs. Source: https://www.investopedia.com/terms/m/mercantilism.asp

know that the false hope of the economic efficiency of the business/government alliance (fascism) was, in effect, a fascist lie. Government cannot do, through coercion, what free people can do through capitalist laissez faire. Government can only gum up the works and make free trade impossible. (Consider this as you examine ESG) (Parenthesis mine)

"Once Germany began confirming (through concentration camps and genocide) the murderous nature of fascist nationalism, and in particular, its desire to grow through military acquisition in the leadup to the Second World War, Americans and Brits began to see fascism in a different light. The American leftists, seeking to shed the guilt of being associated with fascism, tried to exonerate themselves for their duplicity with fascism. This fed the growing power of pragmatism to manipulate citizens and turn them into "voters" duped into creating the perception that society would be improved by capitulating to the lies that the end justifies the means and "some sacrifices had to be made" in order to build the future promised by the coming central government.

"Yet, the concept of fascism, in the form of the "modern" government/business alliance, did not die after the war. We are living under the government/business alliance as we write. Certainly, it was Hillary who declared her advocacy of the … business/government alliance, while her allies in the Democratic Party called Trump the fascist. He too had no problem with pragmatism."[43]

---

[43] "Left versus Right – a False Choice" by Robert Villegas https://amzn.to/3zJtV6L (Paid link)

The Call to Sacrifice as a Destroyer of Society

Something sinister is affecting the minds of many men. It involves a particular method of thinking that is habitual. I identify it as "the call to sacrifice". Not only is it a habit, but it is also a gaslighting gimmick. As a habit, it represents the *internalization* of human sacrifice, and as a gimmick, it represents the method of *normalizing* human sacrifice.

The gimmick is simply this: The altruist leader, as social agitator, identifies something "wrong" and declares an emergency that people must act upon immediately. The agitator then declares that the emergency is so dire that we must organize altruistic giving around it to mitigate the damage and punish the perpetrators of the emergency.

The cause of the emergency is often capitalism and/or egoism (selfish people); the solution to the emergency is always collective action that *everyone* is beholden to engage in (ritual human sacrifice). In other words, the solution to the declared emergencies is always ritualized collective action (socialism, voluntarism, and the mixed economy).

This "so-called" problem solving gimmick is intended to insinuate altruism into society while also denigrating and legislating against self-interest, individual rights, and freedom. This gimmick also evades the fact that man survives by using his mind; and the act of corralling men into "groups" of mindless followers also invalidates their minds.

I have seen this gimmick in action. I have seen people "collected", so to speak, and required to give up values in order to solve the problems that caused an alleged emergency. Altruists depend on guilt and collectivism in order to manipulate people into sacrificing their values for others. Altruism and collectivism have been insinuated into society for millennia of human societies. Men are constantly looking to identify emergencies in order to manipulate people into joining forces to "solve" those emergencies. Every time a so-called emergency comes up, the shaman collectivizes individuals and insists that they sacrifice their deepest values to solve a problem that is supposedly besetting the tribe. In fact, this ritual of human sacrifice is one of the long-standing rituals of human history.

I quote from another book presently being written: "Insinuation is another form of incrementalism that involves the piecemeal repetition of a lie (sometimes called "The Big Lie"). Insinuation can also work to hide the premise that some people are considered evil for wanting to live in a self-interested way. For instance, collectivism can be insinuated by constantly repeating ideas that glorify sacrifice to the collective. To accomplish this, they use terms such as "working together," "sacrificing for our fellow men," "it takes a village" (and more), all of which imply that sacrifice to the collective is moral."

Below is a description of the four ages of social development in which collectivism and tribalism are insinuated into society.

The First Age of Sacrifice - Tribal Age of Altruism – Stone Age:

A. The shaman, in this case, must first indoctrinate the members of the tribe into believing that the way to security is for every individual to believe that they should be sacrificed (killed) to appease menacing gods. This is done through what I call insinuation of sacrifice as good.

B. The shaman educates the tribesmen to submit their minds to his dictates. This, in effect, destroys the ability of the individual mind to act separately and forces him to capitulate to every collective solution brought forward by the shaman. In this way, the shaman enshrines collectivist thinking as a constant state of mind.

C. The shaman enshrines human sacrifice and declares the means for selecting a scapegoat who will be sacrificed for the sake of the gods or society.

D. The scapegoat is identified and incarcerated in preparation for the sacrifice. This is done

through the ritualized meeting that joins each member of the tribe who must participate in the killing of the scapegoat.
E. The day of the human sacrifice is set to coincide with a past event that involved either catastrophe or destruction of some type.
F. Prayer to the god is engaged as the community is enlisted to worship and ameliorate the god's attacks on the village.
G. The people gather to beseech the god to save the people through the killing of human life – the death of the scapegoat that is presumed to be the cause of the coming catastrophe. The scapegoat is almost always someone who is beautiful, individualistic, or self-interested (not willing to sacrifice).
H. At this event, the scapegoat is ritually killed as a metaphor for the life of the god.

The Second Age of Sacrifice - Human Sacrificial Rites Become Morality – Bronze Age:
A. The shaman has firmly established among the collective that self-sacrifice is good morality. Morality becomes religion.

B. The shaman has added animals and goods to the mix. All of these are confiscated on a regular basis and used as scapegoats.
C. Narratives based upon the movement of the skies are converted to narratives of the lives of the gods that are imprinted into the minds of the citizens. Society is now built on religion while the citizen looks for every opportunity to prove that he is a good sacrificial animal. He looks for approval in each face he sees.
D. The ritual reenacts the life of the sacrificial god and his death for the sake of the group.
E. Men in tribal societies were only capable of "believing" what they were told and obeying their masters. These were the first "conditioned" men who felt they had no choice about what they should do.

The Third Age of Sacrifice - Morality as Metaphor/Allegory – Iron Age:
A. The altruist leaders have firmly established themselves among the society by consistently teaching that self-sacrifice is a benevolent moral principle for guiding society.
B. The leaders of society claim the right to dispose of individual lives and put them to

the service of society. If he or she is an artisan or tradesman, they claim his product. He or she is their slave.

C. Now, men have religion to remind them of their moral duties on behalf of other men. Religion is comprised of two fundamentals, first, the nature of reality as floating abstractions and second, the nature of man's mind is educated to believe rationalizations and false concepts intended to rule their minds.

D. Altruism has become the modern form of human sacrifice. It is no longer connected to ritual but to ethics and morality, to actions required of individuals on behalf of society.

E. Psychologically, men are conditioned to think of others first and give no thought to themselves. This started with the very first human sacrificial rites and continued through each phase of altruism.

The Fourth Age of Altruism – Modern Society and Modern Philosophy – Modernity

A. All the principles of past societies have been insinuated into modern society by religion and modern philosophy. Individuals in society have accepted the Kantian notion of duty as the moral categorical imperative.

Kant also declares that the "noumenal world (the real world) was made up of things that cannot be perceived while things in the phenomenal world are not real and consist of distortions and "filters" from the collective mind that creates reality. ... Man's mind shuts down. Kant shuts the world off from the mind and made it stochastic in nature – random. The result is institutionalized human sacrifice, the legal implementation of the idea that sacrifices must be made for the sake of society. You are the sacrificial victims of …Kant." (See the previous chapter)

B. The ancient ritual of human sacrifice has become taxation, expropriation of property, and genocide. The leaders of society have become skilled manipulators of the minds of man, to such an extent that average citizens are trained to obey and think of themselves as virtual slaves to society. They cannot think for themselves without rejecting Kant's indeterminacy.

C. Due to the influence of Kant and modern philosophy, a secular morality called altruism has taken the role of ritual human sacrifice. It's other name, thanks to Kant is "Duty" that Kant calls a "categorical imperative" derived from the collective mind.

D. Philosophy has converted rationalism, concrete-bound thinking, and the anti-conceptual mentality into a new form of the old religion based upon the Kantian analytic-synthetic dichotomy that took over and weakened men's minds.

E. Altruism is a morality derived from Kant's metaphysics and epistemology. Men think they are doing good when they give up their values and accept the roles of sacrificial victims as a matter of their citizenship.

F. Men whose minds have been indoctrinated by modern philosophy lose their abilities to be independent thinkers. Like their religious counterparts in earlier ages, they don't have the ability to think for themselves and this makes it easier for their leaders to convince them to follow their instructions.

These four ages of the development of civilization reveal that, unfortunately, two of the common denominators of many civilizations have been altruism and collectivism as they work in unison to enslave mankind. Although altruism and collectivism are not the only characteristics retained by each system, it is altruism, especially that has degraded each age and led to some of the most notorious and murderous events in history.

The Art of Killing Men

How does a man come to the decision to kill another man? What is it within a man that brings him to killing another?

There are two types of human killing. The first is the termination of a human life by means of force or violence. A man kills a man by using a weapon of destruction. Needless to say, the victim is considered by the killer to be unworthy of life. This is almost always a subjective valuation made without logical deliberation, or it could be a valid logical justification based on a proven act of evil or a tangible danger posed by the victim.

I'm reminded of the protagonist of Dostoevsky's *"Crime and Punishment", Raskolnikov* who describes his future victim as a "spiteful old widow" whose apartment had "not a speck of dust to be seen". This observation made by the young man was a clear indication of spite and jealousy toward someone he valued very little, or should I say, someone he hated because she was not him. After pawning a watch to the old lady, he tells himself:

""Oh, God, how loathsome it all is! and can I, can I possibly... No, it's nonsense, it's rubbish!" he added resolutely. "And how could such an atrocious thing come into my head? What filthy things my heart is capable of. Yes, filthy above all, disgusting, loathsome, loathsome! — and for a whole month I've been..."[44]

Certainly, he was thinking about robbing the lady, having learned that she kept valuables in a locked drawer in her flat.

Dostoevsky declares Raskolnikov, the young man, to be a monomaniac, that is, a man obsessed by one thing, which, based upon the writer's presentation of him in Chapter Two, must be the obsessive fear of having people around him. In modern terms, this would be an "agoraphobic psychology" which is a person afraid of crowds, the basis for strong inclination toward anger and hate towards others under certain circumstances. In other circles, Raskolnikov exhibits characteristics of schizophrenic psychology.

Yet, he uses a second strategy to help him execute his plans. It involves manipulating the mind of his victim in order to incapacitate her and keep her from realizing his plans for ending her life. He exhibits traits such as cleverness and careful planning. We see him inventing his own axe to kill his victim. He plans to hide the axe in his clothing and to commit the crime while the victim is alone and totally within his control. Likewise, he hides his most powerful weapon, knowledge, from his victim. He plans to isolate her so she can only obtain her knowledge from him. When it is

---

[44] Dostoyevsky, Fyodor. Crime and Punishment. Pandora's Box. Kindle Edition.

time to make the kill, the victim has no choice but to succumb to the plan of the killer.

You may not have noticed that the above paragraph is also a description of the traditional and primordial relationship between altruism and the self-sacrificial victim in the religious rite of human sacrifice that I have written about in this book. Let us see the connection. I will slightly edit the paragraph above to make my meaning clear: "Yet, the primordial altruist also plans on killing the mind of his victim in order to incapacitate her and keep her from realizing his plans for ending her life. He exhibits traits such as cleverness and careful planning. We see him inventing his own moral "axe", altruism, to kill his victim. He plans to hide the axe using guilt to commit the crime while the victim is alone and totally within his control. Likewise, he hides his most powerful weapon, knowledge, from his victim. He plans to isolate her so she can only obtain his knowledge from him. When it is time to make the kill, the victim has no choice but to succumb to the plans of the killer."

As we can see, altruism can kill too and it can be used consciously and willfully by the altruist to manipulate his victim, steal from him, and kill his plans for his own life. Altruism is a form of killing individuals and, over time, it kills millions in the form of genocide justified by the government that corrals people and sends them into the pit.

Yet, the altruist is a weakling, a willful destroyer of human life. Dostoevsky describes him thusly: "His hands were fearfully weak, he felt them every moment growing more numb and more wooden. He was afraid he would let the axe slip and fall... A sudden giddiness came over him. ""But what has he tied it up like this for?"" the old woman cried with vexation and moved towards him.

"He had not a minute more to lose. He pulled the axe quite out, swung it with both arms, scarcely conscious of himself, and almost without effort, almost mechanically, brought the blunt side down on her head. He seemed not to use his own strength in this. But as soon as he had once brought the axe down, his strength returned to him. The old woman was as always bareheaded. Her thin, light hair, streaked with grey, thickly smeared with grease, was plaited in a rat's tail, and fastened by a broken horn comb which stood out on the nape of her neck. As she was so short, the blow fell on the very top of her skull. She cried out, but very faintly, and suddenly sank all of a heap on the floor, raising her hands to her head. In one hand she still held "the pledge." Then he dealt her another and another blow with the blunt side and on the same spot. The blood gushed as from an overturned glass, the body fell back.

He stepped back, let it fall, and at once bent over her face; she was dead. Her eyes seemed to be starting out of their sockets, the brow and the whole face were drawn and contorted convulsively."[45]

Like Raskolnikov, the altruist is quick to "kill" the mind and ensure he cannot escape the clutches of the philosophy of altruism. The victim has no choice but to submit.

In my book, *"Nihilism and its Role in the World"*[46], I defined nihilism as "...the realization of the worst conclusion of the most explicit interpretations of the worst thoughts. It is banality expressed as normality, hiding undercover. Nihilism is the idea that advances the destruction of all values until nothingness rules all of existence. Any idea that even partially seeks to destroy values and good is nihilism. Therefore, altruism and collectivism and progressivism are all nihilism; they are the Kantian nightmare of switched meanings and lies built upon lies. Nihilism is the re-distribution of all good for the sake of all evil. Likewise, altruism is the child of nihilism. We saw this with Raskolnikov, and we see it also in Camus' character Meursault.

---

[45] Crime and Punishment by Fyodor Dostoyevsky https://amzn.to/3Osy4mG
[46] https://amzn.to/3tnIUDP

"The term "nihilism" is derived from the German Nihilismus which is from the Latin nihil ("nil, nothing") added to the German -ismus ("-ism"). It was coined in 1817 by German philosopher Friedrich Heinrich Jacobi.
"If modern philosophy preaches that man knows nothing, that he is dirty and corrupt, then a strict nihilism is the worst conclusion of the worst thinking; that man is the lowest form of creature on a planet of the worst creatures possible. If the "cur" (the altruist) is taught that men are evil, he will consider it his duty to destroy all men at every turn. He chooses the words which will actualize his worst conclusions."[47] (parenthesis mine)
Likewise, the connection between killer and victim can be seen in Camus' book, *The Stranger*"[48].
Camus provides the context through which the philosophy of existentialism is built.
Existentialism is the philosophical justification for nihilism that pretends to be the "truth."
Existentialism tells us that nothingness is just the way the world is; that nothingness is all that man can achieve.
Albert Camus, although not an admitted existentialist, displays this sense of life in his

---

[47] Nihilism and its Role in the World by Robert Villegas https://amzn.to/3ethYHm (Paid link)
[48] https://amzn.to/46FZjl4

novel. Camus' style and exposition provide an eloquent fictional declaration of existentialist views.

EXISTENTIALIST METAPHYSICS

Camus' philosophy appears to begin and end with metaphysics, with a view about the nature of the universe and man's relationship with it. His hero, Meursault, a young Frenchman, is attending his mother's funeral. Like Dostoevsky's Raskolnikov, Camus' Meursault possesses an unusual and dispassionate attitude. He vacantly goes through the motions one is supposed to go through at funerals. One senses that Meursault does not care one way or the other, that for him, his mother's death is simply an occurrence, something that happened.

After the funeral, he returns home and meets a young girl friend named Marie. They spend a few days swimming and relaxing, after which time she asks him to marry. He replies that he "didn't mind," that if she was keen on it, they would. It really didn't matter to him.

Camus establishes Meursault's attitude toward the universe at the outset. Nothing really matters. Nothing is of importance. Our hero feels this from the beginning, and he practices his feeling by declaring that nothing really matters to him.

Later, after Meursault's conviction for murder, Camus encapsulates his concept of certainty by bringing the hero face to face with death, the goal for which he had lived. Meursault describes his conversation with a priest:

"Then I don't know how it was, but something seemed to break inside me, and I started yelling at the top of my voice. I hurled insults at him. I told him not to waste his rotten prayers on me; it was better to burn than to disappear. I'd taken him by the neckband of his cassock, and, in a sort of ecstasy of joy and rage, I poured out on him all the thoughts that had been simmering in my brain. He seemed so cocksure, you see. And yet none of his certainties was worth one strand of a woman's hair. Living as he did, like a corpse, he couldn't even be sure of being alive. It might look as if my hands were empty. Actually, I was sure of myself, sure about everything, far surer than he; sure of my present life and of the death that was coming. That, no doubt, was all I had; but at least that certainty was something I could get my teeth into—just as it had got its teeth into me. I'd been right, I was still right, I was always right I'd passed my life in a certain way, and I might have passed it in a different way, if I'd felt like it. I'd acted thus, and I hadn't acted otherwise; I hadn't done x, whereas I had done y or z. And what did that mean? That, all the time, I'd been waiting for this present moment, for that dawn, tomorrow's or another day's, which was to justify me. Nothing, nothing had the least importance, and I knew quite well why. He too, knew why. From the dark horizon of my future a sort of slow, persistent breeze had been blowing toward me, all my life long, from the years that were to come. And on its way that breeze had leveled out all the ideas that people tried to foist on me in the equally unreal years I then was living through. What difference could they make to me, the deaths of others, or a mother's love, or his God; or the way a man decides to live, the fate he thinks he chooses, since one and the same fate was bound to 'choose' not only me but thousands of millions of privileged people who, like him, called themselves my brothers. Surely, surely, he must see that. Every man alive was privileged; there was only one class of men, the privileged class. All alike would be condemned to die one day; his turn, too, would come like the others.' And what difference could it make if, after being charged with murder, he was executed because he didn't weep at his mother's funeral, since it all came to the same thing in the end?"

Camus' hero is caught up in a universe poised against life, in a hostile, malevolent, and yet indifferent wind. Reality struck this man full-fisted. There was no escape, not in life, not in death. He had liberated himself from all that had been "foisted" upon him and he saw it all as fake and meaningless. His view is that life had been malevolent towards him, and he saw no reason to angrily express his confusion and hatred of all the people he had relied upon; a mother, a life, a priest, and lots of lies.

Camus, himself an atheist, is using his vehicle, Meursault, to crash into religion and, in the process, express his own malevolence toward mysticism. Existentialism is *existential*, but it deals in universal dis-value. It is nihilism and not religion, per se, that is the spiritual target. The existentialist hates religion because it exhibits some features of positive morality and metaphysics just like many nihilists today. In this sense, Camus, the existentialist believes religion represents false values, a false notion; and, because so, he obliterates the floating abstractions found in religion's rationalist base. His is a hatred of religion on an existentialist base.

EXISTENTIALIST EPISTEMOLOGY

Epistemology studies theories of knowledge, theories of how man develops and organizes the material obtained from his sensory contacts with reality. Existentialism, as a philosophy, necessarily has views about how man knows, but, in a sense, the philosophy is a self-canceling system. In a sense, it cancels itself by holding that man obtains his sense of knowledge automatically without any effort. If man seeks knowledge through existentialist doctrine, he will learn that the effort is fruitless. And, in a sense, this is the same effort that Raskolnikov made to control the mind of his hapless victim. This is killing a man by killing his mind. It is the same tactic as the shaman who controls the minds of his tribal victims.

Novels, of course, only express epistemological theories through the thoughts of characters in narrative, their reactions to the things that happen to them. Rarely does a novelist hold an explicitly developed epistemological framework. He merely describes his characters' thoughts. Yet, we find in Camus's writing an almost explicit development. Meursault is a receptacle. He makes no effort to learn, yet he begins with one premise: it is not necessary. Meursault merely floats through life with his basic knowledge always obvious to him. An excellent example of Camus' epistemological views is found in the murder scene. Meursault and his friend Raymond had just faced a group of Arabs who were intent on killing Raymond. A confrontation had occurred on a beach, and the Arabs had fled, after which Meursault and Raymond returned to the bungalow where they had guests:

"When we reached the bungalow Raymond promptly went up the wooden steps, but I halted on the bottom one. The light seemed thudding in my head and I couldn't face the effort needed to go up steps and make myself amiable to the women. But the heat was so great that it was just as bad staying where I was, under that flood of blinding light falling from the sky. To stay, or to make a move—it came to much the same. After a moment I returned to the beach, and started walking.

"There was the same red glare as far as eye could reach, and small waves were lapping the hot sand in little, flurried gasps. As I slowly walked toward the boulders at the end of the beach I could feel my temples swelling under the impact of the light. It pressed itself on me, trying to check my progress. And each time I felt a hot blast strike my forehead, I gritted my teeth, I clenched my fists in my trouser pockets and keyed up every nerve to fend off the sun and the dark befuddlement it was pouring into me. Whenever a blade of vivid light shot upward from a bit of shell or broken glass lying on the sand, my jaws set hard. I wasn't going to be beaten, and I walked steadily on.

"The small black hump of rock came into view far down the beach. It was rimmed by a dazzling sheen of light and feathery spray, but I was thinking of the cold, clear stream behind it, and longing to hear again the tinkle of running water. Anything to be rid of the glare, the sight of women in tears, the strain and effort—and to retrieve the pool of shadow by the rock and its cool silence!

"But when I came nearer I saw that Raymond's Arab had returned. He was by himself this time, lying on his back. His hands behind his head, his face shaded by the rock while the sun beat on the rest of his body. One could see his dungarees streaming in the heat. I was rather taken aback, my impression had been that the incident was closed, and I hadn't given a thought to it on my way here.

"On seeing me, the Arab raised himself a little, and his hand went to his pocket. Naturally, I gripped Raymond's revolver in the pocket of my coat. Then the Arab let himself sink back again, but without taking his hand from his pocket. I was some distance off, at least ten yards, and most of the time I saw him as a blurred dark form wobbling in the heat haze. Sometimes, however, I had glimpses of his eyes glowing between the half-closed lids. The sound of the waves was even lazier, feebler, than at noon. But the light hadn't changed; it was pounding as fiercely as ever on the long stretch of sand that ended at the rock. For two hours the sun seemed to have made no progress; becalmed in a sea of molten steel. Far out on the horizon a steamer was passing; I could just make out from the corner of an eye the small black moving patch, while I kept my gaze fixed on the Arab.

"It struck me that all I had to do was to turn, walk away, and think no more about it. But the whole beach, pulsing with heat, was pressing on my back. I took some steps toward the stream. The Arab didn't move. After all, there was still some distance between us. Perhaps because of the shadow on his face, he seemed to be grinning at me.

"I waited. The heat was beginning to scorch my cheeks; beads of sweat were gathering in my eyebrows. It was just the same sort of heat as at my mother's funeral, and I had the same disagreeable sensations—especially in my forehead, where all the veins seem to be bursting through the skin. I couldn't stand it any longer, and took another step forward. I knew it was a fool thing to do; I wouldn't get out of the sun by moving on a yard or so. But I took that step, just one step, forward. And then the Arab drew his knife and held it up toward me, athwart the sunlight.

"A shaft of light shot upward from the steel, and I felt as if this blade transfixed my forehead. At the same moment all the sweat that had accumulated in my eyebrows splashed down in my eyelids, covering there with a warm film of moisture. Beneath a veil of brine and tears my eyes were blinded. I was conscious only of the cymbals of the sun clashing on my skull, and, less distinctly, of the keen blade of light flashing up from the knife scarring my eyelashes, and gouging into my eyeballs.

"Then everything began to reel before my eyes, a fiery gust came from the sea, while the sky cracked in two, from end to end and a great sheet of flame poured down through the rift. Every nerve in my body was a steel spring and my grip closed on the revolver. The trigger gave, and the smooth underbelly of the butt jogged my palm. And so, with that crisp, whipcrack sound, it all began. I shook off my sweat and the clinging veil of light. I knew I'd shattered the balances of the day, the spacious calm of this beach on which I had been happy. But I fired four shots more into the inert body, on which they left no visible trace. And each successive shot was another loud, fateful rap on the door of my undoing"

Every novelist communicates both epistemological and metaphysical views implicitly by means of his exposition; and Camus is no exception. In fact, he is an expert wordsmith in this respect. One will notice that Meursault seems so affected by the universe around him that he is totally incapable of rational thought, that, in effect, he is not thinking. In a situation of this sort, knowledge of a usable kind is impossible, and the only knowledge possible is unusable. Camus seems to be saying that although man can think, the universe makes it extremely difficult.

On the other hand, it is clear from the events of the murder in this book, that Meursault was cognitively impaired and fuzzy-minded. He saw everything through a distorted filter that matched a cognitively disabled mentality.

EXISTENTIALIST ETHICS

The same scene will serve to illuminate Camus' ethics. Because the universe is poised against life, and because this is the only certainty, we must conclude that any action based upon "the ideas that people tried to foist on" Meursault is false; that no ethics will apply to man since he can do little about the more overpowering wind of the universe. Meursault borrows the old cliché, "it's common knowledge life isn't worth living anyhow."

In effect, this view that life isn't worth living, is the goal, the end toward which existentialism moves. Although Existentialism is not a true philosophy, it mimics a true philosophy, nevertheless. Any time men drop metaphysics and epistemology, their only resort is to pragmatism, to action without mind and to knowledge without certainty, both of which lead to mindless action and dependence upon the minds of others; and this dependence is the starting point for altruism and its deadly consequences. The idea that nihilism and altruism are evil should have come to men over a long development, but the existentialists could not wait for the final destruction of philosophy. They wanted to affect it immediately. The end, which is nihilism and its child altruism, was the goal.

EXISTENTIALIST POLITICS

According to nihilism, the state is a sham, an unnecessary convention devised to stifle the individual, a corrupt organ made of hatred and ritual.

What is one to do about it? Submit to the agents of nihilism by submitting to the state? These agents rule reality, and their opinions lead the minds of those dependent upon them. This is the sacrifice of the individual mind to the collective mind, otherwise known as democracy/socialism/communism. It is to this "collective mind" that Meursault gives up his life which is why he ends by blaming his defaults on the collective (the others) he has always worshipped. You cannot convince them of their absurdity, he thought, knowing they would eventually inflict capital punishment upon him. After all, here, in Meursault, is the man who murdered another without any motive, almost totally unaware that he was doing it, and in the final analysis, at the mercy of a cause beyond his control that he both hated and worshipped. How could one possibly convince the fools that he is innocent, that the universe is poised to destroy him regardless of what he does? How absurd is the state to try determining such unnecessary drivel as laws when it cannot possibly know the true nature of things by any means?

EXISTENTIALIST PSYCHOLOGY

From the start, Camus sets a mood that is carried through to its logical nihilist conclusion. The story picks up after Meursault had been counseled by a priest. The novel rises to a crescendo of despair and ends with the same quiet noncommittal attitude:

"Once he'd gone (the priest), I felt calm again. But all this excitement had exhausted me and I dropped heavily on to my sleeping plank. I must have had a longish sleep, for, when I woke, the stars were shining down on my face. Sounds of the countryside came faintly in, and the cool night air, veined with smells of earth and salt, fanned my cheeks. The marvelous peace of the sleepbound summer night flooded through me like a tide. Then, just on the edge of daybreak, I heard a steamer's siren. People were starting on a voyage to a world which had ceased to concern me forever. Almost for the first time in many months I thought of my mother. And now, it seemed to me, I understood why at her life's end she had taken on a "fiancé;" why she played at making a fresh start. There, too, in that Home where lives were flickering out, the dusk came as a mournful solace. With death so near, Mother must have felt like someone on the brink of freedom, ready to start life all over again. No one, no one in the world had any right to weep for her. And I, too, felt ready to start life all over again. It was as that great rush of anger had washed me clean, emptied me of hope, and, gazing up at the dark sky spangled with its signs and starts, for the first time, the first, I laid my heart open to the benign indifference of the universe. To feel it so like myself, indeed so brotherly, made me realize that I'd been happy, and that I was happy still. For all to be accomplished, for me to feel less lonely, all that remained to hope was that on the day of my execution there should be a huge crowd of spectators and that they should greet me with howls of execration."[49]

Moral crisis today most often results from the inability of an individual to live up to the requirements of "duty", otherwise known as altruism. Yet, this "crisis" is not a moral crisis – but a good thing. Men should not be criticized into thinking that there is something morally wrong in the act of defending themselves from the "takings" of altruism. They should be proud of it. This purported moral crisis is opposed to any act or thought of the individual's self-interest.

In fact, the goal of altruism is to begin the process of "killing" the individual, to compromise him (or her) morally. The practice of killing man's mind is accomplished by criticizing everything he or she thinks about personal relationships (messing them up), the requirements of sacrifice (giving up), the evil of self-interest (hating himself), and anti-individualism (not standing up for himself),

---

[49] Note: Permission for use of excerpts from "The Stranger" by Albert Camus (Translated by Stuart Gilbert) was grant by Alfred A. Knopf, Inc. Copyright 1942 by Librairie Gallthart as L'Etranger. Copyright 1946 by Alfred A. Knopf., Inc.

that would disorient his or her basic physical and intellectual needs. The analog to these "mind games" is to preach the philosophy of nihilism, including the hatred of values and the hatred of the individual.

Putting men into the position of being unable to focus and respond to these negative attacks must result in the deaths of both minds and bodies. Self-destructive ideas cause self-destructive and unavoidable acts, all in the name of saving altruism and nihilism. Altruism, collectivism, and nihilism are the tools used for the murdering of individuals. They destroy freedom, values, morality, society, and the future of mankind, and they make the individual the victim of the long-term effect of efforts to destroy his ability to defend himself on moral grounds. The true moral crisis is the advancement of altruism and its negative impacts on human freedom and happiness.

The individual who learns to hate values seeks a mindless rebellion, so to speak, and this creates further guilt and relationship troubles. Values represent a form of moral knowledge. They are concepts for which the individual strives. To tell men to give up their values is an effort to destroy the moral knowledge that he needs to survive and to achieve moral certainty. This is why you see Raskolnikov and Meursault move slowly from valuing the innocents around him to hating their "values" (including their lives) to the point of destruction of life.

The dominance and overwhelming power of altruism, combined with the act of criticizing people for not sacrificing, combine to create tremendous pressure on the individual; and this pressure is never acknowledged by the culture though it is everywhere. You feel it when the priest talks about man's "sinful" nature, when you are asked for a donation by some charity or loved-one, when you are criticized for being selfish (or when you criticize others for being selfish), when politicians talk about higher taxes on the wealthy (or the middle class), etc. When leaders declare that "anti-fascists/fascists" are correct when they kill thousands or millions, you are being taught hatred of values, hatred of individuals, hatred of freedom, and hatred of "selfish" morality, you are being taught to hate man's sense of being moral. All of these nihilist, altruist, and collectivist notions that we are being taught today add up to the statement: "I am not moral, and they hate me for it." The result is the ultimate genocide that not only destroys bodies but also minds. "Be careful of the dark." Always remember that when society kills minds, eventually it will kill bodies. In order to kill the body, altruism must first kill the mind.

Conclusion: Learning to Live Outside of Altruism

As I have written: The stochastic frame of mind inaugurated by modern philosophy (Hume and Kant, et al) is an intellectual collapse that infects the human mind and creates random leaps into misunderstanding, faith, magic, collectivism, altruistic morality, and misguided social action.

While rationalist impediments work to undermine objective thinking (thinking about reality) the minds of men become littered with religion (faith), collectivism (socialism, communism, etc.) and altruism (self-sacrifice), etc. Their personal lives become dominated by a social demand that men lower their expectations and accommodate people without high values who become the enemies of man's happiness. That is what they must be if men are to be slaves to society. A separation between virtues and values corrupts their living and makes them the victims of thieves, robbers, and politicians.

Kant bequeathed menticide, the killing of the mind, human ignorance, and immorality by preaching that man's mind was incapable of connecting to the real world (and effecting reason), independence and self-interest. Since Kant's demise, mankind has been infected with not knowing what to think, how to think, what to do and how to decide what to do. In fact, the mental state that Kant bequeathed to mankind, is the state of a mind in default. The only cure for this insanity is to reject modern philosophy and proceed according to reason.

Learning how to reason and how to create a proper moral code has become man's greatest challenge in the wake of Kant' call to duty. Man starts by learning about the proper methods of thought by embarking upon 1) a new epistemological framework of human learning, 2) ascertaining the metaphysical framework of the real world, 3) making the connection between morality and politics, 4) and finally knowing the connection between virtue and value.

This new approach to human thought and morality would save mankind if he were to embark on a new mission of philosophical reasoning. This would bring the true Independence Day.

Additionally, man must learn to recognize when human thinking has strayed from its proper course. He must recognize the influence of Kant and his corruption of thinking and morality. He must recognize the influence of rationalism, religion, collectivism, and altruism; and, most importantly, he must recognize when a deadly poison has been introduced into the human mind.

Whenever men hear the appeal to human sacrifice, they must learn to oppose it, to argue against it, and to present the antidote that will defeat the illogical appeal to sacrifice and slavery. That antidote includes human reason, individual rights, and logical discourse that liberates the pursuit of happiness. The true difference is that between freedom and slavery.

Learning to live outside of altruism means being vigilant about the anti-mind mantra being preached today. This mantra seeks to denigrate the human mind and prepare the way for the acceptance of evil as a human solution. That evil is the call to kill men for the sake of society under the idea that the end justifies the means and perception is reality. It is the call for men to altruistically sacrifice all values for the sake of a faux social cohesion.

Against this call, men must become vigilant and resist the gaslighting, lies, and coercion of the centralized state. Men must struggle to attain the knowledge needed to rebel against the wretched ideas of altruism, collectivism, genocide, death, and pragmatism. It is the call for men to live outside of the mental prison of indeterminacy and insanity. Instead of anti-conceptual thinking, men must resort to the independent mind that has learned to think for itself and resist the call to sacrifice in favor of the call to reason.

About Robert Villegas

Robert Villegas is an American writer born in Weslaco, TX. He is an independent philosopher with a strong focus on the practical consequences of ideas. He considers the philosophy of ideas to be a central factor in creating a better society and he offers both a critical discussion of modern philosophy as well as practical solutions and fundamental principles to solve problems associated with pragmatism and indeterminacy. His work stands on its own.

Mr. Villegas spent over twenty-seven years as a UPS executive in Indiana and worked in locations all over Europe such as Germany, England, and Spain. At UPS he worked as a Call Center Manager and Telecommunications Manager. He was involved in helping to transition UPS from paper-based processes to computerized networks and digital record keeping. He worked with early digital technologies and was one of the first telecommunications managers to develop a system for communicating to drivers while they were on their routes.

After leaving UPS, Mr. Villegas started his own sport marketing company specializing in writing sponsorship proposals for race car drivers and other athletes. Clients included Johnny Parsons, Jeff Ward, Larry Foyt, and Alexander Rossi to name a few. He also worked as a technical writer in the burgeoning telecommunications industry in South Florida where he created many successful sales presentations and marketing documents. He also built his company's first website and worked for companies throughout the country including New York City, Boston, San Francisco, Sacramento, Chicago, Miami, Minneapolis, Vancouver BC, and other locations.

In 2015, he began to pursue his life-long goal of becoming a published author and has written about 109 books to date in areas such as novels, theater, religion, poetry, philosophy, and business. During this period, he also wrote over 260 Business Plans mostly for companies in Canada. He also wrote grant proposals and developed grant proposal narratives for several organizations, earning millions of dollars for fire departments and charitable organizations.

He has also served in the US Military as a communications specialist and served his tour of duty during the Vietnam era in Korea near the DMZ. He was raised in Indiana and presently lives in Arizona.

He was educated in Indiana and earned a Degree through the University of the State of NY (Albany) via an external degree program when he came out of the military. He is divorced with three grown children and three grandchildren. Famous relatives include Mexican anti-hero Dimas DeLeon and guitarist and music producer Johnny Garcia of Weslaco, TX

Alcoholism and Addiction – the System

These four books comprise a system that can be used by both patients and counselors who are battling Alcoholism and Addiction. Based upon Mr. Villegas's own system developed during his struggle against alcoholism, this system includes:

Alcoholism and Addiction – A Secular Ten-Step Program
This groundbreaking book offers a secular approach to alcoholism unlike that offered by Alcoholics Anonymous. We recommend that every individual going for alcohol and drug-abuse counseling be given a copy of this book which contains the workbook and the two versions of The World's first drunk. http://amzn.to/2md6R9w $3.45 Kindle $11.95 softcover

The Secular Ten-Step Program Workbook
This booklet covers the program developed by Mr. Villegas. It is designed as a workbook with blank spaces for the patient to write his own thoughts as he takes each of the ten steps. Order one copy for each patient in counseling. http://amzn.to/2lrHimS $4.49 Kindle $6.95 softcover

The World's First Drunk – With Counselor Talking Points
This booklet is designed for the counselor as he works with patients during individual or group therapy. It contains helpful tips on discussing the life story of the man who invented alcohol. Order one copy for each patient in counseling. http://amzn.to/2l446Wr $2.99 Kindle $5.95 softcover

The World's First Drunk – Patient Version
This version of the short story contains empty spaces where the patient can answer questions about the life story of the man who invented alcohol. Order one copy for each counselor. http://amzn.to/2ldxBGb $2.99 Kindle $5.95 softcover.

Books on Christianity

Unkilling Jesus
Who was Paul and what was his role in the creation of Christianity? What was his provenance, and did he meet the resurrected Christ? Who wrote Revelation and what was the document's purpose? Why was Domitian assassinated? http://amzn.to/2itMCo0 $3.99 Kindle $15.95 softcover

Domitian: The Final Messiah
The central goal of this book is to define the specific themes and concepts that make up Domitian's contribution to Christianity – in a sense, we are defining the specific Domitian overlay to the Christian materials originally developed for Titus. http://amzn.to/2yWMSlx $2.99 Kindle $6.95 softcover

Paul's Agon and the Mystification of History
Paul and Jesus are joined in one important way; the way of a miracle. They met on the road to Damascus while Paul supposedly pursued Christians. Jesus, in a sense, told Paul to get with the program and stop persecuting his people. In this incident, the Bible tells us that Jesus is already dead, and resurrected. This book argues otherwise. http://amzn.to/2zSDsuP $5.99 Kindle $19.95 softcover

Christianity on the Arch of Titus
This book explores the "persons" visible on the Triumphant Arch of Titus which is located in the heart of Rome. These people were significant in that they played a role, not only in Rome's conquest of Judaea but also in the creation of Christianity. This book explores those individuals and the roles they played in the creation of one of the most important religious movements in world history. https://amzn.to/3xz3OgM $3.69 Kindle 10.95 paperback

Books on Religion

The Mark of Titus
Excerpts from the book Unkilling Jesus which highlight some of the key discoveries implied by new theories about the origin of the Jesus Myth. The idea that the Romans invented Christianity is the basic premise of new theories about the origin of Christianity.http://amzn.to/2itMCo0 $3.49 Kindle $5.95 softcover

Contra Religion
This book is designed as a "shorter" explanation of the ideas presented in my larger book, "Behind the Ritual Mask" which seeks to define fundamental principles of religion. I'm hoping this book will serve as a primer for the original book and spur an interest in reading it. http://amzn.to/2yWMSlx $3.99 Kindle $6.95 softcover

Is this the Face that Launched a Thousand Ships?
It was love at first sight. I saw her one day while watching a television program about King Tut, whose tomb had been discovered by Howard Carter years before. I was looking at the famous bust of a beautiful Egyptian Queen. https://amzn.to/3t487x3 $3.99 Kindle $7.95 softcover

The History of Altruism
The History of Altruism is a historical treatment of the development of altruism throughout time from the Paleolithic period to today. It tracks the development of self-sacrifice of primitive man to the advent of altruism as a development from Kant's "duty". It covers a broad sweep of concepts and shows how they influenced modern man, religion and societies through the ages. https://amzn.to/3gN8zgy $4.19 Kindle 14.95 paperback.

Values and Purpose Books by Robert Villegas

The Real Purpose-Driven Life
After centuries of being told that it is not about you, it is time to set the record straight. You are a unique individual and your goal in life should be to achieve your own happiness. This book is about helping you accomplish your goals and fixing your purpose firmly in place. It covers not only why you should pursue your goals but how to do it. https://amzn.to/3ebkhjr
$3.99 Kindle $6.95 softcover

The Values and Purpose Workbook
Rather than give you tasks that involve doing a lot of things for other people, I'm am going to tell you that focusing on yourself will reveal your life's purpose and express your passions and freedom. I'm going to start with you. https://amzn.to/3eQf4wG $2.99 Kindle $6.95 softcover

This Book is About You
Some people move briskly bent on a purpose, concerned only about what they are about. People walk by them; they don't even notice. They just keep to their path and you wonder where they are going. This book is about you. It's about time. https://amzn.to/3vFMzss $6299 Kindle $5.95 softcover

Self-Help Books by Robert Villegas

Existence a Rational Thoughtbook
A Rational Thoughtbook is designed for thinking as opposed to reading. It combines brief prescient content with stunning imagery. Existence focuses on the nature of existence and gives you intelligent thoughts to integrate into your life.
https://amzn.to/2RZpsKV $4.99 Kindle $12.95 softcover

The Virtue of Independence
One of the most important goals for any person is to establish intellectual independence. Intellectual independence is the road to "life" independence, which is the ability to earn your own way without help from others. https://amzn.to/3awuCV2 $2.99 Kindle $6.95 softcover

Rational Meditation
Rational Meditation is self-meditation. It is thinking about yourself without guilt and without the tenets of modern philosophy (that the world is unknowable, that man is a phony, that ethics and living are only about others). https://amzn.to/3gus9OE $6.99 Kindle $12.95 softcover

History of My Mind
This booklet is the companion to my book entitled Rational Meditation. It utilizes the various exercises of the original book that involve contemplation or meditation and provide space for written input by the reader. https://amzn.to/3gy3hpl $4.69 Kindle $11.95 softcover

Rational Thoughtbooks by Robert Villegas

 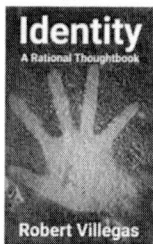

Existence a Rational Thoughtbook
A Rational Thoughtbook is designed for thinking as opposed to reading. It combines brief prescient content with stunning imagery. Existence focuses on the nature of existence and gives you intelligent thoughts to integrate into your life.
https://amzn.to/2RZpsKV $4.99 Kindle $12.95 softcover

Identity
One of the most important goals for any person is to establish intellectual independence. Intellectual independence is the road to "life" independence, which is the ability to earn your own way without help from others. https://amzn.to/3nf9aJn $3.99 Kindle $9.95 softcover

Fiction and Creative Poems and Plays

   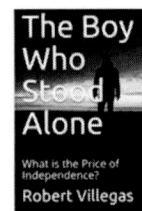

Poetic Prose and Poetry
These expressions represent some of Mr. Villegas' deepest thoughts as he lived and traveled throughout the world in locations such as Germany (East and West), Austria, Britain, Spain, Canada, France, Luxembourg, Belgium, the Netherlands, Korea, New York, Miami, San Francisco and other locations. https://amzn.to/3vu7X3B $2.99 Kindle $6.95 softcover

The Lost Poems
These poems were discovered among Mr. Villegas's archives in 2016. Many of them have been read by only Mr. Villegas. Most of these poems were rejected as "not that good". After seeing them again, he has changed his mind. These poems expressive, fresh and spontaneously honest. https://amzn.to/3aPg5nB $3.99 Kindle $6.95 softcover

Adam Reborn – A Short Play
Adam Reborn is a play of symbols. Adam and Eve, as I have portrayed them, are young and heroic people learning to deal with a Paradise and God that are hostile to them. There is no chance of life for them. https://amzn.to/3u9Nr8b $2.99 Kindle $6.95 softcover

The Boy Who Stood Alone
Jonny Payne has just discovered Ayn Rand and his parents don't know what to do. They take him to a priest and a psychologist but his only question is "What is the price of independence? https://amzn.to/3nCG6ve $3.99 Kindle $6.95 paperback.

Fiction and Creative Materials

Aphrodite
Johnny is a Spanish guitar player with a mysterious past. At a party, he meets the beautiful songstress Aphrodite who is enthralled with his flamenco guitar skills. Later, she learns they have a connection, a particular song they both appear to know. Aphrodite discovers the connection, and through dreams, the two fall in love. The question is whether they will ever be together. https://amzn.to/3xIlmXZ $3.99 Kindle $5.95 softcover

The Odyssey of Amerigo the Founder
Amerigo was born in a time of desperation and dystopia. He was the only man with the vision of a great future. Many repaired to his cause while others swore to destroy him. They wanted his life, his mind and everything he loved. He swore that no matter what they did, he would win the struggle for freedom and a new future. https://amzn.to/2Qz8h2t $3.99 Kindle $8.95 softcover

Bob and Bobbie
1967 - a town outside Camp Casey, Korea - two young people have come together to challenge a world that makes love impossible. https://amzn.to/3sZWSpf $2.99 Kindle $5.95 softcover

The Raven Haired Girl
Bobby met Angie 52 years ago in a poor neighborhood in Indianapolis. It was love at first sight. For a few short months, their relationship blossomed into love. They were in love but didn't know how to be in love because they were only fourteen years old. https://amzn.to/3306plF $2.99 Kindle $6.95 paperback.

Other Books by Robert Villegas

Naming Names in the NT
"Discovery consists of seeing what everybody has seen and thinking what nobody has thought." - Albert Szent-Gyogyi – 1937 Nobel Laureate
https://amzn.to/3mXR66H $3.99 Kindle $9.95 softcover $16.95 hardcover

Finding Your Soft Cry
Every individual has a yearning to know that he is both free and good. This yearning comes to him from early youth, and he hopes that he eventually develops the intellectual tools to help him distinguish between his nature and the demands of society. The key to freedom is the ability to act without restriction and, especially, without guilt. https://amzn.to/3p8lY7m $3.99 Kindle $8.95 softcover $15.95 hardcover

The New Totalitarianism – Quo Vadis?
The previous century was one of the bloodiest in history. Two World Wars and many other wars do not bode well for our century that is beginning to rival the previous in its bloodlust. If we look carefully, we find in the last century the philosophical roots of the present century. The philosophers of the last century are the philosophers of the present. https://amzn.to/3AMZNFC $5.99 Kinde $10.95 softcover $25.95 hard cover

A Call to Reason
Is it possible that the problems in the world are not caused by capitalism and rich people? Is it possible that anti-capitalism and anti-reason philosophies are nothing more than elaborate hoaxes designed to convince people to give up everything they have honestly earned and take it away from them? Is it possible they are caused by the re-distribution of capital to wasteful uses and the consequent destruction of jobs and affluence? https://amzn.to/3mVNrq5 $5.99 Kindle $9.95 softcover $24.95 Hardcover

Poems for the Stage

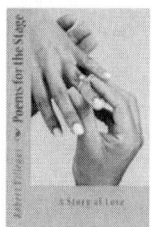 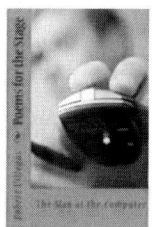

Poems for the Stage – A Story of Love
This dramatic presentation features poems found in Mr. Villegas's book Poetic Prose and Poetry. Some are also found in his book.
https://amzn.to/3gSJctV $2.99 Kindle $5.95 softcover

Poems for the Stage – The Man at the Computer
This dramatic presentation is based upon poems from Mr. Villegas's book Poetic Prose and Poetry. Some of the poems have been slightly altered to reflect the internal story. Mr. Villegas's book Poetic Prose and Poetry can be found on Amazon.com.
https://amzn.to/2R8zpFf $2.99 Kindle $5.95 softcover

More Books on Politics and History

A Boomer takes on the Far Left
I just learned something about myself – and it isn't very good. In fact, it is very bad. I learned that the opinions of Boomers don't matter any more. We are obsolete in this new age of new knowledge. Anything we think is unimportant and false. I don't think so. https://amzn.to/3tzNqtc $5.19 Kindle $10.95 softcover

Crushing the Alinsky Radicals
The worst enemy of individual rights today is a group of people I call the Alinsky Radicals. These people are now in charge of our culture and temporarily, in charge of government. They are associated, philosophically and politically, with the communists and fascists of the past. They are not your father's liberals. They are the direct descendants of dictators such as Stalin and Mao. In this book, I hope to convince you of the evil of the Alinsky Radicals and to provide the intellectual ammunition you need to eradicate them from society.
https://amzn.to/3hbh9WN $3.49 Kindle $8.95 softcover

The Conservative's Dilemma
I wrote this book to ask some important questions about the conservative philosophy of altruism. https://amzn.to/3bfDQ8e $2.99 Kinde $6.95 softcover.

The Biggest Mistakes in History – 2008 to 2016
To be the Chief Executive of the greatest country in the world requires a leader with a great deal of knowledge, experience and reasoning ability. It requires having the very best minds as advisors, minds that the President can count on to give reasoned arguments and detailed knowledge about the important issues of the day. I think it takes a special ability to understand the principle of cause and effect concerning how government action impacts the lives of real people.
https://amzn.to/3tDQ4Ol $2.99 Kindle $10.95 softcover

Books on Politics and History

Dachau and Berlin in 1990
This booklet chronicles Mr. Villegas' thoughts during visits to Dachau and Berlin during 1990, disclosing my observations of milestones in German history, past and present, and relating those events to world happenings as they were unfolding at the time. I traveled throughout Germany for much of 1990 while on business. https://amzn.to/3ex578d $2.99 Kindle $6.95 softcover

What Harvard and Princeton Don't Want You to Know
The professors at Harvard and Princeton don't want you to know about the worst ideas in history. This is because they have been pawning these ideas off as true and profound. They have been using them to deceive and manipulate us for centuries. https://amzn.to/3farP5p $5.19 Kindle $9.95 softcover

Defending American Values
This book is made up of several chapters about American values and how they can be defended without a descent into the abyss of dictatorship. The book argues for individual rights and provides reasons why we should fight for them. https://amzn.to/3uMFq9L $3.99 Kinde $5.95 softcover.

Capitalism Doesn't Fail
How many times have we heard the old saw: "Capitalism has failed again" over the course of contemporary events? We heard it during the Great Depression of 1929 after Hoover had invoked tariffs and precipitated economic retaliation and a banking crisis. Along with this question usually came a statement to the effect, that "We can fix capitalism and make it even stronger by issuing economic controls or spending money to stimulate economic activity." This book will argue that capitalism, as an economic system, cannot fail as long as individuals are free to act. https://amzn.to/3xZIAJ6 $4.19 Kindle $10.95 softcover

Books on Psychology and Virtue

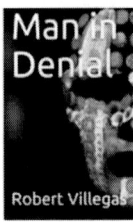   

Man in Denial
If psychology has no solid epistemology and metaphysics, how can it stand on its own? I do not think it can and this explains why psychology is in such a sad state today. Yet, before we can put psychology on a solid foundation, philosophy too must advance above the level of puberty. With its base in modern philosophy, even philosophy cannot stand on its own which exposes the real problems with modern psychology. https://amzn.to/3oVTDAQ $5.99 Kindle $9.95 softcover $18.95 hardcover

Understanding the Modern Mind
The purpose of this book is to delve into critical issues about how the human mind has come to the modern position of doubt and despair. The culprits in this matter include the irrationality of both rationalism and skepticism, and, in particular, the child of skepticism known as pragmatism.
https://amzn.to/3mRLZF9 $6.99 Kindle $9.60 softcover $26.95 hardcover

How Marcuse Destroyed Capitalism
One of the fathers of critical theory was Herbert Marcuse who escaped European dictatorship only by coming to America. America gave him the freedom and protection he needed to destroy capitalism in America.
https://amzn.to/2YW9LaS $4.99 Kinde $8.95 softcover.

The Logical Fallacy of Altruism
A logical fallacy is a faulty thought process that violates a rule of proper thinking. Correct arguments are defined as proper generalized expressions that define logical truths or knowledge. In effect, a rule of logical reasoning addresses all of the common modes of valid argument while the faulty argument contradicts them. This book examines altruism as a logical fallacy.
https://amzn.to/3vdFiB0 $5.99 Kindle $9.95 softcover $18.95 Hardcover

Books on Sport and Entertainment Sponsorship

Finding Sponsors 1 and 2
This book is written for anyone seeking sponsorship relationships in the sport and entertainment fields. The ideas and principles presented here are applicable to any company, sport team, entertainment company, marketing agency and charitable organization that uses corporate sponsorships to support its activities. Volume 1: https://amzn.to/3ejm1Hp $5.19 Kindle $12.95 softcover Volume 2: https://amzn.to/3eVDo0e $4.69 Kindle $10.95 softcover

How to Write a Sponsorship Proposal
This booklet provide you with some basic guidelines on what to communicate in order to produce a winning sponsorship proposal. These guidelines will focus on what you should be presenting to your potential sponsor to make the best business case for involvement with your team or entertainment company. $2.99 Kindle $6.95 softcover

Hospitality Event Planning Handbook
One key part of your sponsorship activation strategy might be customer hospitality events in conjunction with sporting events. How do you pull off a Hospitality Event for your biggest customers? You may not know how to start, what to do and how to ensure the event is a success. This book can help. http://amzn.to/2mxzpgy $7.95 softcover.

Selling Sponsorship in the Age of the Coronavirus
This book provides suggestions on how sport teams, athletes and concert promoters can mitigate the damage done to their businesses by the economic lockdowns (due to the Coronavirus). It integrates checklists, SWOT Analysis and other valuable business aids into one toolkit that will help you keep your sport and/or genre alive in these difficult times. https://amzn.to/2QVBNiM $5.15 Kindle $5.95 softcover

Books on Sponsorship and Business

Finding Sponsors Forms Book
This "Forms Book" is intended to provide samples of the forms mentioned in my book "Finding Sponsors for Sport and Entertainment". This will make it possible for you to reproduce these forms in other formats as well as download the forms document from the SponsorProAZ website for use with Microsoft Word. https://amzn.to/3b95yDW $2.99 Kindle $5.50 softcover

Submitting Your Sponsorship Proposal Online
This booklet enables sport teams and concert promoters to submit their sponsorship proposals to companies that accept only online submission of proposals. https://amzn.to/3euzdti $2.99 Kindle $5.95 softcover

The Art of Sponsorship
This short book is based upon Mr. Villegas' book "Finding Sponsors for Sport and Entertainment". It is also based upon a course that he taught for an organization managing Indiana Parks and Recreation facilities. It is, in a sense, a condensation of information from the book geared toward organizations that would like to earn revenues on their facilities through corporate sponsorship.
https://amzn.to/3beuVnC $2.99 Kinde $6.95 softcover.

Restarting Your Business After the Pandemic
This new book is designed to help you restart your business after the Coronavirus pandemic. You will find here all the right questions, how you can find the answers and the forms you need to walk through your restart and coming success. https://amzn.to/2QVBNiM $5.15 Kindle $5.95 softcover

Manufactured by Amazon.ca
Acheson, AB